DAILY RUNNING WITH JESUS

ELIZABETH MINIKEL

LIGHT SWITCH
PRESS

Published by:
Light Switch Press
PO Box 272847
Fort Collins, CO 80527

Scripture Quotations are taken from the Holy Bible, New International Version, NIV Copyright 1973, 1978, 1984, 2011 by Biblica, Inc.

JANUARY 1ST A NEW YOU, A NEW RUN

And whatever you do, whether in word or deed, do it all in the name of the Lord Jesus, giving thanks to God the Father through him. (Colossians 3:17 NIV)

Today is the start of a new year and you know what that means… an opportunity to make a change! First, congratulations on becoming a runner and choosing to be a better, fitter, and healthier you! Whether this is your very first day running or you have been running since you first learned to lace your shoes, you have a challenging and exciting road ahead of you!

Secondly, but most importantly, thank you for desiring to grow in your relationship with Christ! Your prayer, your hope, and your confidence for this year should be to run and live in a way that brings glory and honor to God. As with any run, there will be times of struggle and times of triumph, but remember no matter what, God is with you every step of the way. God loves you so much more than you could ever fathom or understand and He desires to have a relationship with you! Together, let us run through this year giving God the glory, in everything we do!

JANUARY 2ND GO, FEET, GO!

Then I heard the voice of the Lord saying, "Whom shall I send? And who will go for us?" And I said, "Here am I. Send me!" (Isaiah 6:8b NIV)

You are ready! Ready to run! Like a caged up animal, you have been held hostage in the house all day and you are ready to break free! Energetic feelings of exhilaration and anticipation bubble and overflow inside you as you crouch down to lace your shoes. You open the door and jump over the step, its go time!

You know what? It's go time for all of us! Up! Off the couch and grab your shoes. God has called each and every one of us to go! We get to live our lives for Christ! We are given the opportunity to spread the love of Christ. Tie those shoes; it's time to get busy!

JANUARY 3RD A ROCKY START

"And whoever does not carry their cross and follow me cannot be my disciple." (Luke 14:27 NIV)

Lingering in the hallway? Finding yourself clinging to the doorframe stubbornly refusing to start your run? You glumly stare down at your shoes like a bad cold. The couch looks so much more inviting. Much more comfy and cozy! Even the thought of running sounds ridiculous! Tiring! Downright exhausting!

Following Jesus and doing His will can feel much the same way. It is so much easier to come home from work, collapse into a cozy chair, and glue yourself to your TV. Unless the people you are trying to reach miraculously appear in your living room, it might be a little difficult to tell them about Jesus! It can be uncomfortable, uneasy, and even frightening to obey God's will but He calls us to be faithful servants. Faithful servants willing and ready to do our assignments! Do not fear and do not fret you can do it! Just put one foot in front of the other and get busy today!

JANUARY 4TH RUNNING ABOVE AND BEYOND

Finally, be strong in the Lord and in his mighty power. (Ephesians 6:10 NIV)

Your heart races as sweat pours down your face. Your shoes pound methodically against the hard pavement. You are in the thick of a mountainous climb, straight up and down with nowhere to hide. Your focus isn't on the climb. Nope, you are looking beyond! Up and over the hill lies your destination, your place of rest. The prize of sweet rest lies just beyond the sweat, heart thumping, and achy legs!

Facing a hill in your life? Perhaps you are feeling flat out- out of breath and ready to give up! You are tired. Achy! However, instead of focusing on the nitty-gritty of your current debacle, you press on because you find your strength in the Lord! With God you don't have to focus on the wind and the waves of life but on His outstretched hand. When you zone out the noise and focus, you can hear God's voice calling you, leading you! God's voice assures you of His peace, His love, and an everlasting joy that can only be found in Him! Find your strength in the Lord; knowing that through Him, you can triumphantly get up and over the mountains in your life!

JANUARY 5TH A GEM OF A RUNNER

For you created my inmost being; you knit me together in my mother's womb. I praise you because I am fearfully and wonderfully made; your works are wonderful, I know that full well. (Psalm 139:13-14 NIV)

You are valuable! Did you know that? You, yes you, are a child of God! You are a treasure, a precious jewel, both inside and out. You are worth so much! You are beautiful in God's eyes no matter what you do or don't do. Regardless of how much you run, how much you weigh, no matter what you say or do; God loves you! You are precious to Him.

God lovingly created you. God loves you so much that He sent His one and only Son to take your place on the cross. Your Creator loves you that much! Thank God that you do not have to prove yourself to anyone! Run within God's freedom knowing that you are a precious child of God!

JANUARY 6ᵀᴴ CHOSEN FOOTSTEPS

"For if you remain silent at this time, relief and deliverance for the Jews will arise from another place, but you and your father's family will perish. And who knows but that you have come to royal position for such a time as this?" (Esther 4:14 NIV)

Your footsteps can be found all over your home town. You can discover your shoe prints up and down the quiet streets. You can trace your footpath around subdivisions and trailing down sidewalks. You are a chosen child of God and you have been called for a very special mission, to reach those around you for Jesus!

Your footprints and your handprints are interlaced within your community, within your families, and among your friends for a reason. We were made to tell others about the Messiah! You were chosen for such a time and such a place as this! You are called to witness to the people around you and at all of the places your feet hit the ground! You were handpicked by your Heavenly Father to reach the very people you rub elbows with every day! If you, a called servant of the Lord, don't reach the people you call your family, friends, and neighbors with the gospel, who will? Your feet were not only designed to run but to carry the good news of great joy!

JANUARY 7ᵀᴴ RUNNING PAST THE LABELS

Great is our Lord and mighty in power; his understanding has no limit." (Psalm 147:5 NIV)

Have you been labeled? Have you ever been called slow, unfit, lazy, a quitter, or inexperienced? Those words don't only hurt our confidence but slow us down! But wait! Don't let the labels of others box you in! You are so much more!

We serve a God who is mighty in power and unlimited in understanding! God's power, God's might, and God's love for us far exceeds our understanding! As devoted followers of the one true King, let's live like His children! Be bold and confident to do the will of our Heavenly Father just as He created us. Use the noteworthy skills, talents, and abilities your Creator uniquely gave you to live life to the fullest! So what title is limiting you? What is holding you back from accomplishing your potential? Don't let the words and opinions of others hold you back! No way! Believe that through God, you can run past the labels others stick on you! Be who God has called you to be!

JANUARY 8TH RUNNING ALL HUFFY AND PUFFY

"In your anger do not sin": Do not let the sun go down while you are still angry," (Ephesians 4:26 NIV)

You are irritated. It's written all over your face. The pink fury blazing from your cheeks is not from running hard but from running mad! You aggressively pump your arms and narrow your gaze. Your anger acts as energy to feed your run. You finish in record time but are still holding on to the dismay you left your house with. You are mad and you are not going to let this go!

In life, how often are we willing hold unto our anger? Anger is a heavy bag to carry around. It's cumbersome, toilsome, and heavy on our backs. You cannot run around with all this weight tying you down! Ask your Heavenly Father how to forgive, to let go, and to heal your heart that has been deeply hurt!

JANUARY 9TH MISTAKEN IDENTITY

For you died, and your life is now hidden with Christ in God. When Christ, who is your life, appears, then you will appear with him in glory. (Colossians 3:3-4 NIV)

Your identity is not found within the number of miles you run. Your identity is not defined by your fastest run or by the number of races you have won. Your identity is not even upgraded by your unwavering work ethic, your strength, or determination. None of these things define who you are! Your identity cannot be defined by your earthly bank account, your worldly possessions, your job, or even by your family. No, your identity is found in Christ and in Christ alone!

You are saved by the blood of Jesus and His perfect sacrifice. Not because of anything you have done or could ever do, Jesus accomplished it all on the cross! Jesus is so worthy of all our honor, praise, and glory! Out of the outpouring of love that God has for us, we are able to show the love of God to others! Run to tell others the joyful treasure of love you have found in Jesus!

JANUARY 10TH RUNNING DOWN THE WINTER BLUES

I love those who love me, and those who seek me find me. (Proverbs 8:17 NIV)

Brrrrr! Brrrr! Brrrr! Your teeth chatter loudly inside your mouth. The frigid wind snaps against you, leaving you shaking inside your shoes as you noisily stomp along the white snow covered sidewalk. The powdery snow catches a free ride under your running shoes as it clumps to the bottom of your feet.

"I'm almost home, I'm almost home," you assure yourself as you run as fast as you can to get inside of your warm, cozy front door before you turn into a snowman!

Experiencing the winter blues? Not only are the running conditions proving difficult due to the cold, ice, and snow but the shorter days and longer nights force those outside runs to a treadmill! As the warmness of a thick, soft, cozy blanket and a steaming hot cocoa lure us to sit in a chair, use your longer evenings wisely! Put down the TV remote, snuggle up to the welcoming fireplace, and pick up your Bible. Spend time in the wonderment of your Father's arms as you read his love letter to you. Warm body and soul as you find yourself lost in God's goodness, love, and grace!

JANUARY 11TH PRAISEWORTHY RUNNING

Let the message of Christ dwell among you richly as you teach and admonish one another with all wisdom through psalms, hymns, and songs from the Spirit, singing to God with gratitude in your hearts. (Colossians 3:16 NIV)

Boom! Boom! Boom! You rhythmically run to the beat of the banging drum, methodically vibrating in your ears. You raise your hands in admiration! You feel your skin prickle with excited goose bumps. You sing, really sing, in your heart a song of worship to your God and King.

Put a little skip into your joyful step! That's right, sing a song of praise while you run! Not just any song, a homemade song, which you create to worship your Creator! While you run today, take the beat you are listening to and improvise with heartfelt lyrics that speak of God's goodness, mercy, and grace! Create unique words that come from the heart that speak of the awesomeness of our God! Make a beautiful noise to your Savior and King!

JANUARY 12TH WHERE'S YOUR BUT?

I tell you, now is the time of God's favor, now is the day of salvation. (2 Corinthians 6:2b NIV)

You might have run this winter but...man it was cold! You would have run this spring but... way too much pollen! You tried running this summer but...whoa it was hot! We can be quite inventive when it comes to reasons not to run, can't we?

We come up with a lot of buts! Do you have a but when it comes to serving God? Like you would serve or spend more time with God but...

We constantly talk ourselves out of doing stuff until the right time. But the time to live for Christ is right now! Today is the time to live for God! Now is the time to serve, start a new Bible study, invite your neighbor over for dinner, or go on a mission trip! Now! Forget about your old buts and focus on today and what you can do with the time God has given you! Start running for Jesus today! No more buts about it!

JANUARY 13TH FINISHING THE RUN YOU STARTED

Now finish the work, so that your eager willingness to do it may be matched by your completion of it, according to your means. (2 Corinthians 8:11 NIV)

Your elaborate, well meaning plan has fallen by the wayside. Again! Every year you eagerly plan a well thought out training program to finish a race, but somewhere between family, your job, and free time, your good intentions ... your training has fallen off track! More often than not, our thoughtful ideas and plans disappear right in front of our eyes. We become busy, unfocused, and discouraged. There can be a multitude of reasons to blame.

But don't worry you are not alone. We all mess up and we all fall short. This year, instead of letting our goals go up in smoke, let's lace up our shoes, dig our heels in, and turn that dream into something that will glorify God! It might take some sweat. It might take some tears. But you can handle it, you are a runner! You are strong! Through God, you can finish what you started!

JANUARY 14TH RUNNING ON CRUISE CONTROL

The earth is the LORD'S, and everything in it, the world, and all who live in it; (Psalm 24:1 NIV)

Are you running on auto pilot? Running so focused on your music and the thoughts swirling inside your head that you missed your whole run? You ran of course! You just missed your opportunity to appreciate the overflowing blessings of God's creation that were all around you. You failed to breathe in the smells, hear the sounds, and soak in the beauty of God's creation!

How often do we do the exact same thing in everyday life? We live life on cruise control. Just going through life, checking off people and events, like one big to-do list. Have you been so busy that you have missed all the people God has placed in your life, to not only enjoy but point to Jesus? Today is the day to start really living in the moment! Make today the day you seek to enjoy all God has generously placed around you.

Be intentional and fully present with others. Take a step back to see all that God has blessed and continues to bless you with! Throw off the restraints of technology and open your eyes to the faces and smiles all around you!

JANUARY 15TH STEP INTO MY SHOES

And now these three remain: faith, hope, and love. But the greatest of these is love. (1 Corinthians 13:13 NIV)

You never know how far, until you run. You never know how hard, until you try. And you never truly know about another human being, until you have run in their shoes. We can never judge another's life or journey, unless we were to have lived our lives in their shoes.

The bad news is that we can never truly live in another's place. The good news is that Jesus took our place when He died the death we deserved on the cross! Therefore, we are free to openly love those around us because of God's amazing love for us! Today is the day to ask God to fill our eyes with His love and understanding. Pray that we would see others as God sees them, perfect and just as He wants them. Ask that hearts will be opened and aware to the hurts and needs of our brothers and sisters around the world.

JANUARY 16TH RUNNING TO THE SNACK SHACK

As the deer pants for streams of water, so my soul pants for you, my God. My soul thirsts for God, for the living God. When can I go and meet with God? (Psalm 42:1-2 NIV)

Rumble. Grumble. Gurgle, gurgle…

Is that your belly? Loudly reminding you it's time to eat? After a run, it can feel utterly impossible to fill that hollow pit of a stomach. A hungry runner is a crazy runner until they have satisfied their cravings.

What if we craved God like we hunger for our post run snack? What if we were not content until we had our fill of God? What if we had to seek God not just once or twice a week, but like the clockwork of our gut aching for regular meals and snacks throughout the day?

What would our day look like if we put our King first? Put God before all the physical and mental needs. Place our Creator before ourselves, our jobs, running, and even our families. Like the roaring of a starving tummy, seek God ravenously!

JANUARY 17TH WHEREVER MY FEET MAY ROAM

"Have I not commanded you? Be strong and courageous. Do not be afraid; do not be discouraged, for the LORD your God will be with you wherever you go." (Joshua 1:9 NIV)

God is up on a mountain and down beside a roaring sea. God can be found within the quietness of a wooded trail and on the sidewalk of bustling road. God is inside the crowded gym and outside on the lamp lighted road. God is by you as you take your first step, land your first job, and walk down the aisle. God is right beside you as you are delivered life changing news.

God picks you up as you fall. God encourages and cheers you on when you are about to give up! God is with you wherever you go. God is with you in whatever you do. There is no place you run that God won't be there. There is no place too lonely, too dark, or too destitute for God. God can be found wherever your feet may roam.

JANUARY 18TH UNCOMFORTABLE EQUALS RUNNING

Let us not become weary in doing good, for at the proper time we will reap a harvest if we do not give up. (Galatians 6:9 NIV)

Feeling uncomfortable is nothing new to runners! That is what separates us from those with their feet propped up on a couch! Your legs ache, your feet are blistered, your whole body is sore, and you are literally exhausted! Just as there is a comfort cost to running there can be a comfort cost to tell others about Jesus.

We struggle, we sweat, and we worry about what to say and how others might react. Pray today that God would give you the opportunity, the courage, and strength to share the good news of salvation. Ask God that He would give you the words to say! God always blesses when you make the first bold step, no matter how wobbly, unsure, and uncomfortable that might be!

JANUARY 19TH RUNNING FOR THE "PERFECT BODY"

So God created mankind in his own image, in the image of God he created them; male and female he created them. (Genesis 1:27 NIV)

You stare at the pack of runners as they run in sync around the curve of the track. You wish you could be just like them. You wish to look like them, run like them. Runners and non-runners alike share in their pursuit for what the world labels as the quintessential "perfect body".

We try so hard to sculpt our bodies into the image we think will solve our image problems. Guess what? You were perfectly made! By a perfect God! Your Maker created you just as He wanted you to be! Remember you are fearfully and wonderfully made! God intricately wove each and every piece of you and has a plan for your life. Confidently run knowing you are loved by your Maker. Know that God loves you so much that He sent His one and only Son to die in your place! So instead of running after the image of someone else, proudly run just as God created you to be!

JANUARY 20ᵀᴴ "I'LL JUST RUN LATER"

"Therefore keep watch, because you do not know the day or the hour." (Matthew 25:13 NIV)

You eagerly awake, bright eyed and bushy tailed. Today is the day you are going to start running again! You feel great, fresh, and ready! You take a sip of warm coffee and enthusiastically grab your running shoes. You are just about to pull them on when the phone rings…

Hours later your running shoes remain right where you left them, on the rug by the front door. Somewhere between your chatty mom calling, the next door neighbor needing a favor, lunch, picking up the rowdy kids from school, helping with endless homework, cooking and cleaning up dinner, and bath and bed time; running got pushed off again, and again, and again. As runners we reason that we will have time later in our lives to get healthy and work out, sometimes we put running off. We figure we will have time later.

But many people have taken this fatal route when it comes to accepting Jesus as their Lord and Savior? They reason that they will have time later in life once they are not so busy. But we know every day is a gift for God and not to be taken for granted! So do not wait one moment more and leave your life in the balance! Accept Jesus as your Lord and Savior, He's waiting for you!

JANUARY 21ˢᵀ WHO SAID YOU COULDN'T RUN?

Therefore, my dear brothers and sisters, stand firm. Let nothing move you. Always give yourselves fully to the work of the Lord, because you know that your labor in the Lord is not in vain. (1 Corinthians 15:58 NIV)

Look into the mirror. What do you see? Your reflection reveals a beautifully talented and very special individual created by God. But the mirror also unveils our own worst enemy… ourselves! Sometimes we convince ourselves that we cannot accomplish our heart's desires. We tell ourselves we are not good enough, fast enough, or strong enough. We also convince ourselves that God cannot use us. We tell ourselves that we do not have adequate training or poor biblical knowledge. What have you convinced yourself that you cannot do?

Today is the day to stop saying no and start confidently saying yes to the person God has uniquely created you to be! Want to run that race? Ready, set, run! Do you have the desire to go on a mission trip and tell others about Christ? Go and shout it! Go tell that mirror who you are, a special child of God!

JANUARY 22ND RUNNING SEEMED EASY...

"I will give you a new heart and put a new spirit in you; I will remove from you your heart of stone and give you a heart of flesh." (Ezekiel 36:26 NIV)

"I have to do what!" Running seemed like a piece of cake, easy peasy. All you need is an open space, appropriate running shoes, and a pace that exceeds that of a walk. But as you already know, it takes so much more! It takes dedication, heart, and feet that have a passion to go!

Following Jesus also seemed relatively painless. We reason all we have to do is go to church once a week, raise our hands a little, attend a couple of charity events during the year, and stay out of trouble. But following Jesus is less of what is happening on the outside and has everything to do with what's in our hearts. The good fruit that we produce is only a product of the love bearing tree that is growing from the inside. Following Jesus requires a heart change, a life changing transformation! We must trust Jesus as our personal Lord and Savior, and make Him the King and Master of our life!

JANUARY 23RD RUN-INS

Be very careful, then, how you live- not as unwise but as wise, making the most of every opportunity, because the days are evil. (Ephesians 5:15-16 NIV)

Leave room in your run for a "run-in"! A time within your run to make a difference in another's life! Almost every run gives us ample chances; to enthusiastically greet a passerby, kindly open a door for someone, lovingly spend a moment helping a neighbor, encourage a fellow runner, or pause to do whatever it is that God has placed in your path. It's time we viewed our distractions in life as open doors!

Run-ins are perfect opportunities, given to us by God, to point others to Jesus, and to be examples of Christ's love. It's time to stop cramming our days so full that we leave no room for what God has in mind as a possible gift, both for someone else, and for ourselves. When we leave no room for God to work in our lives, every little inconvenience leaves us feeling angry and frustrated. We rob ourselves of joy if we constantly see every person and everything only as a distraction and not as the open door God intended it to be. So leave room for a "run-in" today!

JANUARY 24TH SMELLY SHOES

So in Christ Jesus you are all children of God through faith, for all of you who were baptized into Christ have clothed yourselves with Christ. (Galatians 3:26-27 NIV)

If you had a choice, would you continue to run in your old battered shoes or would you wear the beautiful new shoes you have been perfectly fitted for? New shoes of course! No runner would want to continue shuffling around in a pair of raggedy, stinky and worn out sneakers when they have a brand new pair waiting in their closet!

In the same way, when we accept Jesus as our Lord and Savior, we are made new! We no longer have to walk around in our old and worn out clothes! We are now clothed in Christ! So proudly display the love and grace of Jesus for everyone to see! Tell them why you traded in your rags for riches!

JANUARY 25TH RUNNING FADS

"I the LORD do not change." (Malachi 3:6a NIV)

Eat this! Wait, don't eat this... eat that! Wear these shoes! Hold up... instead wear these shoes! Still yet... do you even want to wear shoes? Fads come and go, especially for runners! One moment, we runners are eating, wearing, and drinking the latest and greatest. The next minute we find ourselves all in on a radically different band wagon!

Change is inevitable. Fads wax and wane, circumstances change, seasons come and go, and our health and bodies weather as time goes on. Only God remains unchanging! Isn't it reassuring to know that although everything in life may change, the God we serve never does? Praise and worship our timeless and unchanging Heavenly Father!

JANUARY 26TH RUNNING WITH DETERMINATION

"But as for you, be strong and do not give up, for your work will be rewarded." (2 Chronicles 15:7 NIV)

Look at you go! Your determination and grit is written all over face. You are driven! You understand all those miles are not going to run themselves! Runners are resolute, undaunted and unwavering by the task at hand. They have to be. Running is indisputably hard. Therefore runners have to be persistent in order to stay the course, to finish the race.

Just as adamant as you are in running, have the same unwavering zeal and tenacity as a follower of Christ. Be determined to live a life that brings glory and honor to God. Be a dedicated example of Christ's love to everyone around you, always pointing others to Christ. Run the race with determination, both for your physical heath and for the race that is everlasting. With your eager diligence others cannot help but see that that fire burning bright inside of you! Shine on!

JANUARY 27TH UNQUENCHABLE THIRST

Jesus answered, "Everyone who drinks this water will be thirsty again, but whoever drinks the water I give them will never thirst. Indeed, the water I give them will become in them a spring of water welling up to eternal life." (John 4:13-14 NIV)

Must… drink… water…now! As a runner, you crave water! Especially on those long, hot runs. Until you get that first drink of smooth, cold water your thirst buds will not be satisfied. Every step you take only reminds you of how thirsty you truly are. Nothing but water can quench your thirst, not lemonade, not hot chocolate, not a coffee, not a diet soda, and not even a milk shake!

Like water to our bodies, our souls thirst to be filled with God! The only thing that can satisfy that longing in our hearts is Jesus. Not a new car, not your spouse or children, not your dream job, and not even a perfect body can fill the spot where Christ belongs in our lives. We need Jesus like our body needs water. Just like our bodies will die if we do not drink, our souls will be eternally lost if we do not make Jesus the Lord and Savior of our life. So drink up and quench your thirst with our Savior who eternally satisfies!

JANUARY 28TH RUNNING REQUIRES LISTENING

And he said to me, "Son of man, listen carefully and take to heart all the words I speak to you." (Ezekiel 3:10 NIV)

Come closer…. a little closer… listen. Do you hear it? It's you! Your body is talking! Telling you what it needs and how it feels. Runners often forget one very critical piece of running: listening. We sometimes push ourselves so hard that we fail to pay any attention to what our body is actually telling us.

Perhaps you are a great body listener and always keep an active ear to how you feel, but how often do you stop and take the time to listen to God, to hear his voice? Sometimes we need not speak, but listen. Concentrate on what God has to say to you within the stillness and peacefulness of His presence! Open your ears to God's loving voice today while He still may be heard!

JANUARY 29TH RUNNING IN THE MOMENT

"Enter through the narrow gate. For wide is the gate and broad is the road that leads to destruction, and many enter through it. But small is the gate and narrow the road that leads to life, and only a few find it." (Matthew 7:13-14 NIV)

Okay you have one second to make a decision! Times up! What are you going to do? Running is jammed packed with split second decisions. Runners make choices again and again that either place their feet on a safe haven or directly in harm's way.

We only are given seconds to make a very real and tangible impression of Christ and who He is in our lives to those around us. But how often do we just let those moments slip by! What will you do with the seconds you are given? Will you chose to use them for Christ or for yourself? Run with each and every moment God gives you to be a witness for Him! Eagerly take advantage of every minute to live for Christ!

JANUARY 30TH BEAUTIFUL FEET

How beautiful on the mountains are the feet of those who bring good news, who proclaim peace, who bring good tidings, who proclaim salvation, who say to Zion, "Your God reigns!" (Isaiah 52:7 NIV)

Raise them up! Yep place those sparkling jewels for all to see! That's right we are talking about your handsome piggies! You, yes you, have beautiful feet! Did you know that? As a runner, the thought of having gorgeous feet has probably never even crossed your mind. Especially since your feet are probably covered with calluses, rough edges, broken and blackened toe nails, and blisters! Not exactly sandal season ready!

But God sees your feet differently. God sees your feet as beautiful! So use those beautiful feet to do more than just run. Employ those wonderful feet to wholeheartedly seek and spread the good news of salvation that only comes through Jesus Christ! Put those feet to a glorious use!

JANUARY 31ST RUNNING UNRAVELED

The LORD is my strength and my shield; my heart trusts in him, and he helps me. My heart leaps for joy, and with my song I praise him. (Psalm 28:7 NIV)

You accidentally slept in. You then proceeded to spill coffee on your new shirt, earn a speeding ticket, and then clock in ten minutes late to work. But your day didn't end there! You later had to endure a hectic work day, get stuck in heavy traffic, and finally arrive home late to a sink full of dirty dishes. Sound familiar? As if everything went downhill the moment you opened your eyes? Did you then make the call to just skip your run altogether and call it a day?

Rough days can make us feel like we have a free pass not to do the things we know we should do. On chaotic days we can find it easy to pass up time with God and miss out on the precious moments with Him that are so vital and refreshing to our soul! Spend that crucial time praying and reading God's Word. Just as important as it is to go out on that run, it is more important to bring your day to God. Drop that bad day at His feet, pick up the pieces and run in God's peace and joy the rest of the day!

FEBRUARY 1ST FAITHFULLY RUNNING BESIDE

A friend loves at all times, and a brother is born for a time of adversity. (Proverbs 17:17 NIV)

You quickly spot them ahead of you! Tucked into the crowd, swinging their arms, and screaming your name! Your pit crew! Your confidant! That person that is always there, every race! Rain or shine. They are always there to motivate you through your training, pick you up when you become discouraged, and nurse you back to health when you trip and fall.

Everyone has that somebody. Who is that somebody to you? Whoever that person or persons might be, take the time today to thank them. Thank them for their loving support and for always being there. Thank them for encouraging you in your faith, holding you accountable when you fall, and cheering you on as you mature in Christ. Thank them for the love they have shown you as you continue to discover and unfold God's love for you.

FEBRUARY 2ND BRAVE RUNNERS

We are therefore Christ's ambassadors, as though God were making his appeal through us. We implore you on Christ's behalf: Be reconciled to God. (2 Corinthians 5:20 NIV)

You are a runner! What an amazing reason to be proud! A wonderful accomplishment! Running requires persistence and perseverance to do it! You are fierce! To be a runner you have to be determined, focused, resilient, tenacious, courageous, and fearless! But more important than your identity in running is who you are in Christ!

Did you know that as a Christian, you bear Christ's name when you run. Yes you! You are an ambassador of Christ! As ambassadors, we have the pleasure of serving as the hands and feet of Christ! Isn't that awesome? We are given the pleasure to be a representative to a King who is loving, gracious, giving, faithful, powerful, compassionate, merciful, everlasting, and forgiving. Who wouldn't want to serve our amazing God? Proudly run and represent!

FEBRUARY 3RD NOT IF, BUT WHEN

"I have told you these things, so that in me you may have peace. In this world you will have trouble. But take heart! I have overcome the world." (John 16:33 NIV)

As you stoop down to tie your shoes, you lace them knowing one thing: at one point during your run, the going will get tough! As runners, we have embraced the inevitable truth of running's demanding strain but we know it doesn't have to stop us!

Why then do we often go through life assuming it will be easy going and pain free? So then when we become injured or suffer loss, we immediately assume God does not love us. We question God's plan for our lives. We start to doubt his goodness and mercy. We become angry and fearful and ask God, why me? However, Jesus never said we would have a carefree life. In fact, Jesus said just the opposite! So what are we supposed to do, not if, but when we have trouble? Trust God! Do not be afraid because The One we trust in is the conqueror of all!

FEBRUARY 4TH RUN IN YOUR OWN SHOES

"Now this is eternal life: that they may know you, the only true God, and Jesus Christ, whom you have sent." (John 17:3 NIV)

Have you ever asked someone else to run for you? Maybe wished someone could run for you! Unfortunately, runners know it doesn't quite work this way! We have to make the decision to run. We have to train. We have to put our shoes to the road if we want the results running delivers. If it was that easy, we probably would all recruit a friend to run for us while we happily spread out on a comfy couch! To ask someone else to run for you sounds quite ridiculous!

However, often as Christians we think we are saved because of someone else's faith and their personal relationship with Jesus. Are you riding on the coat tails of someone else's faith? Who is Jesus to you? Just as unrealistic as it is to ask someone else to run your race is as silly as it is to think we are saved through someone else's faith. So run your own race in Jesus, He desires to run beside you! God wants a relationship with you!

FEBRUARY 5TH I'M NOT HAPPY UNTIL I RUN

My heart says of you, "Seek his face!" Your face, LORD, I will seek. (Psalm 27:8 NIV)

Feeling super grumpy, instantly irritable, or hopelessly moody? Perhaps you were even short with your family, snappy with your co-workers, and beyond agitated with traffic. But then it all turned totally around once you slipped into your running shoes and left your downcast mood in the dust. You are not satisfied until you run!

Experiencing a lack of joy in your day? Turn to God! Until we meet with our Heavenly Father within the pages of His loving Word, we can feel lost, discontent, and desolate. Within the confines of our busy day, we get tossed about, frazzled, and exhausted! As Christians we yearn for the steadfastness and peacefulness that can only be found in God. Without our Master and Creator, we feel unsettled and unsatisfied, until we discover our direction and equilibrium within His embrace. So instead of looking to something or someone else to fulfill your joy for the day, look to Jesus, He is and will always be the answer you are looking for!

FEBRUARY 6TH RUNNING FOR CHANGE

"As you sent me into the world, I have sent them into the world." (John 17:18 NIV)

"Enough is enough!" Have you ever triumphantly said these words? Perhaps you even shouted them! Was it while you were proclaiming these words that you found the strength and motivation to start running? Maybe your epiphany came when you had a health scare that left you knowing it was time for a serious life change.

Are you saying enough to what you are seeing around you? Declaring enough to human trafficking, homelessness, hunger, and preventable diseases? What are you feeling convicted in your heart to say enough to? Be a catalyst for change! Be that difference you desire to see! What breaks your heart and what can you do about it? How can God use you to make a difference in this world for Christ? Pray about it and ask God how He can use you to be a vessel for change!

FEBRUARY 7TH RUNNING NEEDS YOUR SMILE

But the fruit of the Spirit is love, joy, peace, forebearance, kindness, goodness, faithfulness, gentleness and self control. Against such things there is no law. (Galatians 5:22-23 NIV)

Sweat hurriedly rolls down the side of your glistening face. You turn up your lip and square your jaw in deep concentration. You fix your tunnel vision on the road ahead. A runner's determined gaze is not one that emits warm fuzzy feelings to those passing by! But how often do we go around with a cool stare even when we are not running?

Does your everyday personality and mood resemble that of the friendly warm face and open hands that you use to greet others inside church? So even if you are working hard, here is a pretty tough challenge for today: While you are on your run, try smiling to everyone you pass, and give them a friendly greeting! You would be surprised how far a simple smile and act of kindness can go. You never know how a simple glimpse of Christ's love, can inspire someone else.

FEBRUARY 8TH FIT TO RUN

Therefore put on the full armor of God, so that when the day of evil comes, you may be able to stand your ground, and after you have done everything, to stand. (Ephesians 6:13 NIV)

Hydration: check. Energy replacement: check. Your watch: check. Keys to get back in the house: check. Music: check. As runners we expertly arm ourselves with the correct essentials to get the job done. We put our shoes to the pavement, only after we are prepared and ready to conqueror the road ahead of us! As Christians we are also armed and ready for the race that is before us. These special tools, known as the armor of God, allow us to stand our ground against the devil and his schemes.

"Stand firm then, with the belt of truth buckled around your waist, with the breastplate of righteousness in place, and with your feet fitted with the readiness that comes from the gospel of peace. In addition to all this, take up the shield of faith, with which you can extinguish all the flaming arrows of the evil one. Take the helmet of salvation and the sword of the Spirit, which is the word of God." (Ephesians 6:14-17 NIV)

Look at you, you are ready to run, and fitted for battle!

FEBRUARY 9TH PICK UP THE PACE

"For the Son of Man is going to come in his Father's glory with his angels, and then he will reward each person according to what they have done." (Matthew 16:27 NIV)

Two runners run the same route but they run in two vastly different ways. One runner chooses to leisurely jog while the other runner runs with every fiber of their being sweating and breathing vigorously the whole way! The pace to which you run is solely driven by your individual goals.

The question is, in your Christian life, how are you running? Are you running with all your might, giving God your all? Are you zealous and earnest to serve God and others with every precious minute or are you gingerly sauntering around, dragging your feet as you go? God wants to use you! Yes you! You can be used to do God's kingdom work here on earth! The only thing needed is an open heart, willing feet, and useable hands that are willing to be used for God's purpose. Run wholeheartedly for Jesus, making the best use of every moment you are given!

FEBRUARY 10TH BONA FIDE RUNNER

"A new command I give you: Love one another. As I have loved you, so you must love one another. By this everyone will know that you are my disciples, if you love one another." (John 13:34-35 NIV)

It's just moments before your race. You look and feel great! You are fittingly decked out in your very best and most comfortable running gear from head to toe. Just one more finishing touch; so grab the safety pins, make it straight and center, and there you go! Perfect! Your race number is out there loud and proud for all to see! Runners proudly display their race numbers. You would never see a runner hiding it! It's an outward statement of all their hard work, sweat, and tears!

You know what else is an outward statement? Your faith! But do you ever try to hide the fact that you are a follower of Jesus? Do you ever deny that you are a Christian because you wonder if someone will make fun of you or judge you? Live your life in a way that others can see Christ in you. Be an example of God's love for all to see! Proudly display your identity in Christ at the forefront of everything you do!

FEBRUARY 11TH RUNNING IN A PACK

Therefore encourage one another and build each other up, just as in fact you are doing. (1 Thessalonians 5:11 NIV)

Howling for a friend? Are you running as a lone wolf and ready to join a local wolf pack? Looking for a running pack that provides a sense of camaraderie, encouragement, and laughter? Running with others is a great way to stay accountable to your workout and gain that extra push right when you need it most!

Joining a Bible study is a great way to challenge and grow in your Christian faith! Not only will you meet fellow brothers and sisters in Christ but you can learn together, laugh together, and together come to a deeper understanding of just how great our Heavenly Father is! As a fellow group of believers, together you can spur one another on to become closer in your relationship with Christ!

FEBRUARY 12TH RUNNING ON FIRE

When Jesus spoke again to the people, he said, "I am the light of the world. Whoever follows me will never walk in darkness, but will have the light of life." (John 8:12 NIV)

Feeling snuffed out like a heap of ashes where a roaring fire once roared? Has the fiery passion you once had for running fizzled out? Maybe you feel as if your running is not as fulfilling as it used to be, stuck in a precarious rut, missing the thrill you once held.

As a believer we can have days like this too. Maybe you remember that joy, excitement, and wonderment you once felt when you first started following Jesus. You felt unstoppable, as if nothing was impossible! You felt the desire and drive to tell anyone and everyone about Jesus. But now that spark is merely a dim glow. You want Jesus back in your life; you want to feel that fire burning in your soul again. Of course we are not talking about real fire but our desire for Christ! The great news is you still can be a light for Jesus; you just need a fire catching spark from the everlasting Flame. God! That's right, when you tilt your candle and hold it close to the heat of Christ, your flame will not only burn, it will ignite! Be a spark for Jesus and ignite the world for Christ!

FEBRUARY 13TH WAIT, YOU RUN?

And you also were included in Christ when you heard the message of truth, the gospel of your salvation. When you believed, you were marked in him with a seal, the promised Holy Spirit, (Ephesians 1:13 NIV)

Can you say muscles? Whoa! Look at those sculpted running legs! Yep, you've got them! It's easy enough to spot a hardcore runner! If not by their running physique, you can easily identify them by their outfits of brightly colored clothes and speedy shoes! So, how about you? Maybe others, even total strangers, have distinguished you as a runner, but can they tell you are a follower of Jesus?

Do your words and actions point others to Christ? Do others see the love of Christ in you? Can others see and feel the fruit you are producing in Jesus? How can you possibly contain all the wonderful things Christ has done for you? So run and be fruitful! Share with others the wonderful things God has done for you! Give yourself away and give away your hope that is in Christ Jesus!

FEBRUARY 14TH RUNNING IN LOVE WITH JESUS

And I pray that you, being rooted and established

in love, may have power, together with all the Lord's holy people, to grasp how wide and long and high and deep is the love of Christ, (Ephesians 3:17b-18 NIV)

Head over running shoes in love with running? Are you not truly happy until your feet hit the pavement? The love of running is a wonderful feeling, but it does not compare to the amount of love the Father has for us!

Look around, God's love surrounds us! God loves you so much that He sent His one and only Son to be an atoning sacrifice for our sins. So that, through faith in Jesus, we might have everlasting life. Within God's Word, we discover His love on every page. So on a day dedicated to love, take time to meditate and delight in God's love. Run with the love you have for Jesus. With each and every breath He gives you fill your lungs with God's love!

"For God so loved the world that he gave his one and only Son, that whoever believes in him shall not perish but have eternal life." (John 3:16 NIV)

FEBRUARY 15TH UNCLEAR RUNNING

"I have swept away your offenses like a cloud, your sins like the morning mist. Return to me, for I have redeemed you." (Isaiah 44:22 NIV)

Eyes squinting, you carefully run through the thick haze, gingerly making each step as you fumble ahead. Deep morning mists and foggy days prove hosts to suboptimal and even dangerous running conditions.

Like the thickness and darkness of fog, our sins separate us from God. Thankfully, God sent His Son, Jesus to be the redeeming sacrifice for our sins. Everyone who accepts Jesus as their Lord and Savior is forgiven of their sins and guaranteed everlasting salvation. Jesus tore down the wall that once separated us from God! We were paid for with the blood of Jesus, through His death and resurrection.

We are no longer a prisoner to sin and death! Have you made the decision yet to believe in Jesus as your Lord and Savior or are you still lost from God, blindly running through the menacing fog?

FEBRUARY 16TH RUNNING PLAYLIST

Come, let us sing for joy to the LORD; let us shout aloud to the Rock of our salvation. Let us come before him with thanksgiving and extol him with music and song. (Psalm 95:1-2 NIV)

Admit it. You love rocking to your favorite songs! A quick look at your "running playlist" reveals your necessity to run with an extra skip in your step! Listening to tunes while you run can be a major source of motivation! Music is an awesome way to keep up your tempo and another way to really dig into a hard and taxing workout. Jams motivate runners to charge up that mountain, while other melodies peacefully keep us calm and carrying on.

What you are listening to can also determine your mind set. Concentrating on music that is uplifting and positive is a great way to worship God! Even if you cannot sing while running, each word can be carefully pondered, considering each chorus in your heart. So while running, driving, cleaning, or just stretching after a run, let your playlist be uplifting beats from today's Christian musicians or classic favorites that turn your heart and soul to your Savior and King. God is so worthy of our praise!

FEBRUARY 17TH JOYFULLY RUNNING

Do not be anxious about anything, but in every situation, by prayer and petition, with thanksgiving, present your requests to God. And the peace of God, which transcends all understanding, will guard your hearts and your minds in Christ Jesus. (Philippians 4:6-7 NIV)

Run with joy! An overflowing merriment that comes deep down from within your heart! Run with a blissful smile that captures the everlasting gladness you have for all that Jesus has accomplished on the cross and in your life! Focus and concentrate your thoughts and attitude on the joy you have in Jesus!

Replace today's worries and fear with the jubilation you have in Christ! Lay down the heavy problems of the world and firmly hold unto the joyful promises of God! They are all around you, filling you with hope, encouragement, and love! Please run with joy! Running with the love you have in Christ Jesus is the only way to run!

FEBRUARY 18TH RUNNING IN HIS GRACE

For it is by grace you have been saved, through faith- and this is not from your-selves, it is the gift of God-not by works, so that no one can boast. (Ephesians 2:8-9 NIV)

You run with grace filled shoes. You truly do! You have legs that run because of the extravagant grace God has lovingly showered over you. It is by God's grace you woke up. It is by God's grace you are able to put one foot in front of the oth-er. The funny thing is how often we take God's grace for granted. How often we forget to thank Jesus for dying on the cross! The sacrifice Jesus made for us was at the cost of His perfect life.

By grace we are saved. It was nothing we did and it was everything that Jesus already did! There is nothing we can do no matter how big or how small, that can separate us from God's love. So take the time to thank God for the grace He has lavishly poured on you. The beautiful thing is we do not have to do anything to get this grace, all the work was done on the cross. All we have to do is believe! Believe in Jesus Christ as your Lord and Savior and receive God's grace today!

FEBRUARY 19TH RUNNING FOR PRESIDENT

I urge, then, first of all, that petitions, prayers, intercession and thanksgiving be made for all people- for kings and all those in authority, that we may live peaceful and quiet lives in all godliness and holiness. (1 Timothy 2:1-2 NIV)

No matter if we agree or disagree with what is going on in the oval office, we are called as believers to do one very important thing. To pray! Pray for our Presi-dent and their family. Pray that God would bless them, protect them, and use them to bring glory and honor to Him.

As you run today, use this time to pray. Pray earnestly for the President. Pray that the President would use their position in office to make wise and godly deci-sions. Pray also for our nation. Pray that God would raise up bold men and women to share and loudly live out their faith in Christ Jesus. Pray that we would be a nation that seeks God!

FEBRUARY 20TH RUNNING FREE

The Spirit you received does not make you slaves, so that you live in fear again; rather, the Spirit you received brought about your adoption to sonship. And by him we cry, "Abba, Father." (Romans 8:15 NIV)

Shake it off and leave it at the door! Before you head out on your run take a deliberate moment to mentally drop all your negatives! Let go and surrender all your worries, anxieties, fears, doubts and uncertainties. As you run off into the sunset, experience the freedom of letting go! Letting go of everything is easier said than done! We often want to hold close the heavy baggage of the past and fixate on the uncertainties of the future. Once you try this mental exercise during running, try doing it more and more in your daily life.

Instead of focusing on the negative meditate on thoughts that are true, noble, right, pure, lovely, admirable, excellent, and praiseworthy! Let in an influx of good and let go of the things that are not pleasing to God. Drop your cares and worries and accept the peace, love, and joy that only come through Christ Jesus. Run free! Just like your breaths heavily come while running, inhale the good and exhale the bad!

FEBRUARY 21ST READY TO RUN

"So you also must be ready, because the Son of Man will come at an hour when you do not expect him." (Matthew 24:44 NIV)

Always set and ready to run? I bet if I gave you five minutes you would be dressed and ready to rock! Are you always gym bag ready and in a perpetual state of running readiness? Your backpack is set with all your running essentials faithfully waiting to be opened in case you spot a perfect place to run. No matter what, you are always ready to go!

You might be ready to run, but are you ready for Christ's return? Jesus spoke on being prepared for His return because the day and hour is unknown. What will you be doing? Will you be living for God or wrapped in the ways of the world? Will you be wearing your shoes that live for Jesus tied tight and ready to go? Be Christ's hands and feet! Sharing with and caring for everyone around you! Always ready and prepared to share the good news!

FEBRUARY 22ND RUNNING ROCKY ROADS

Do not turn to the right or the left; keep your foot from evil. (Proverbs 4:27 NIV)

You stare mouth gaped, eyes wide in utter amazement at the winding trail ahead of you. Your brain slowly comprehends the fact that you have to run straight up a rocky mountain path. As runners we know not all paths are created equal. Some foot paths are lackadaisical and offer breathtaking serene views, while other routes prove treacherously precarious and vigorous to its passerby.

Life is much the same way. Jesus does not promise us an easy trouble-free and painless life on this earth. Just because we are saved does not mean we are guaranteed a life filled with our heart's desires. What God does promise us is that He will always be there! We will stumble and we will fall, but God is always there to help us! Stay strong and keep the course!

FEBRUARY 23RD TRADING IN YOUR COUCH PANTS

And to put on the new self, created to be like God in true righteousness and holiness. (Ephesians 4:24 NIV)

Leave them right where they lay neatly folded! That's right. Keep those comfortable, loose fitting pants right where they belong…on the couch! Today is a new day, hosting a new you and a brand new beginning. You made a commitment to run, so keep that commitment alive and strong! So let's start our day keeping our new journey at the forefront. As soon as possible, dress in the apparel you intend to run in later, get your running shoes out and intentionally leave them by the door. Have your watch ready, your music out, and your water bottle ready to go!

Becoming a Christian is a life transforming journey! Your old self is being traded in for a new person that is complete with the joy of Christ! You now will spend your life knowing God and making Him known to everyone you meet! As you discover more and more of God's amazing love, how can you not help but share His grace? There is nothing you cannot accomplish when you set your sights on heaven! God is forever for you!

FEBRUARY 24TH RUNNING WITH YOUR BEST FOOT FORWARD

Dear children, let us not love with words or speech but with actions and in truth. (1 John 3:18 NIV)

People are staring! That's right! They are looking right at you! They gaze at you as they drive by in their cars, trucks, taxis, and vans. As a runner everyone sees you! Running creates curiosity and admiration. Why would anyone dedicate so much to an activity that is so grueling? So demanding? So sweaty!

In that same way people examine you in your Christian faith. They are vigilant to what you say, how you interact in both positive and negative circumstances, what you are watching and listening to, and how you treat others. They are eager to inspect how you are different. Are you practicing what you preach? Are you a loud and proud example of Christ's love? Being a follower of Jesus is tough work!

So consider what you say and what you do because you are in the spotlight! Run in a way that points everyone who glances at you to Jesus!

FEBRUARY 25TH TIRED FEET!

"I will refresh the weary and satisfy the faint." (Jeremiah 31:25 NIV)

Are your dogs barking? Your dogs are your feet, and they are barking when they are whipped, sore, and worn out! If you are a runner, then your dogs have probably barked a time or two, or maybe they are not only barking, they are howling! Most especially after a long run!

Are your feet tired from just your everyday life? Maybe your day, your schedule, and your responsibilities are literally wearing you down and out. Between driving here and there, having to be at this activity and that function, along with everything else that needs to be done, you are dog-tired! Bring God not only your barking feet but your weak and weary heart.

Find your source of joy, power, confidence, and strength in an everlasting, ever giving spring of Life. God wants to fill your empty heart with Him! Stop running empty, tired, and sore; and refuel on God's hope and love!

FEBRUARY 26TH RUNNING IN THE DARK

This is the message we have heard from him and declare to you: God is light; in him there is no darkness at all. (1 John 1:5 NIV)

"Oh.... Ouch! Ouch!" You yelp as you stumble in the dark. You didn't even see the tree branch you just haphazardly tripped over. The dark is no place to run. Never! Running in the dark without the proper lighting and gear, can be downright dangerous. You might be running in the dark but are you also living your life in the dark as well?

Are you walking in the light of Christ or hopelessly fumbling around in the darkness of the world? Don't walk but run to the light of Christ! Run to God's loving and protective embrace!

FEBRUARY 27TH RUNNING RAW

But your iniquities have separated you from your God; your sins have hidden his face from you, so that he will not hear. (Isaiah 59:2 NIV)

Swish! Swish! Swish! Swish! Chaffing can feel downright awful! Worse yet, as training goes on the chaffing can get even worse. Before heading out for a run, it's wise to know what spots on your body are more prone to chaffing then proactively treating and preventing those trouble spots.

In our Christian walk it is also important to know your own trouble spots. It is vital to identify those situations, places, and people that can quickly rub you the wrong way and away from God. Is there something that you struggle with that can quickly lead you into temptation? If so find those things and pray for the strength to overcome them. You can do all things through God who gives you strength. You are a new creation; celebrate your new life in Christ!

FEBRUARY 28ᵀᴴ RUNNING UNPLUGGED

In all your ways submit to him, and he will make your paths straight. (Proverbs 3:6 NIV)

Leave it! That's right, take every little gismo and gadget you usually run with and intentionally leave them on your kitchen counter. That includes your music, your watch, your phone, well everything! Today, optimize the soothing silence and peace, to meditate on how good our God is and all that He has done and continues to do in your life. Thank Yahweh for all the blessings He has placed around you.

Soak in the beauty around you and appreciate all the wonderful gifts God has given you. Intentionally immerse yourself in the greatness of your Father, becoming increasingly aware of His closeness and be grateful for His grace. Ask God to open your eyes and view those around you with His grace. Unplug and get lost in your Father's love today!

MARCH 1ˢᵀ SHOES, SHOES, AND MORE SHOES

Now you are the body of Christ, and each one of you is a part of it. (1 Corinthians 12:27 NIV)

Red shoes, purple shoes, blue and green shoes, yellow and white, orange and blue, expensive lime shoes, cheap gold shoes, shoes that sparkle, shoes that glitter, and shoes that accomplish everything short of running the course for you! You overwhelming gaze from one end of the display rack to the other, utterly dumbfounded by the unlimited options. And that's only considering your color options!

Do you ever feel overwhelmed by your options when looking for a church, where to serve, or where to volunteer within the community? There are so many choices! Finding a place to serve and glorify God can at times feel like a shoe shopping experience. So what is the first step? Trying them on and seeing if it's a good fit! Today is the day to go out and explore your options to serve God where He has placed you! You never know what door God is calling you to open!

MARCH 2ND LEARNING THE RUNNING LINGO

But grow in the grace and knowledge of our Lord and Savior Jesus Christ. To him be glory both now and forever! Amen. (2 Peter 3:18 NIV)

"Okay, now you lost me! You are going to do what?" It's easy to become confused over running terms such as intervals, pace, cadence, splits, and taper. Once under the faulty assumption you are just putting one foot in front of the other, you are now forced to learn a brand new foreign language when training!

Have you ever noticed that as a Christian we say words and phrases that non-believers might not understand? As we continue to grow and mature in Christ we begin to hear and use words such as salvation, propitiation, justification, saved, baptism, redemption, and sanctification. When sharing your faith, keep in mind these life saving words might bring confusion to someone who has not heard them before! So when you are sharing the gospel with a friend today, remember to use words and explain terms so they can fully understand the importance of God's life saving words! Share it!

MARCH 3RD A RUNNING START

"See, I am doing a new thing! Now it springs up; do you not perceive it? I am making a way in the wilderness and streams in the wasteland." (Isaiah 43:19 NIV)

Have the desire to run a race? That's awesome! So what's the next step? It's time to find a training plan that fits your fitness level, training needs, and race distance. The great news is you will have so many different running schedules to choose from that map out your plan! Happy Running!

Just like strategically training your body for a race, we need to mindfully stay in God's Word. It's time to get serious and diligent about reading His Word. Just like choosing our running schedule, pick a Bible plan that fits you. Let's keep on track and motivated! This is go-time! Run confidently and live confidently in the person God created you to be!

MARCH 4TH RUNNING WITH GOD

Yet I am always with you; you hold me by my right hand. You guide me with your counsel, and afterward you will take me into glory. (Psalm 73:23-24 NIV)

Reach out your hand. That's right! Open your empty fingers and grab God's hand! Choose to give your run to Jesus. Make a decision to dedicate your run to God. Turn off your phone and leave your music at home. Unplug! Devote your run time to prayer, praise, and thanksgiving to your Heavenly Father. Glorify and honor God with the precious time He has given you.

Now back to your everyday hectic, busy life, what time can you choose to set aside and consecrate to your Heavenly Father? Can you give God your lunch hour, a time where you feast not only on your delicious sandwich but on God's Word? Why not praise God during your daily commute or as you shop in the grocery store, or during your house chores? Will you glorify God while you are on your hands and knees cleaning the floor or wrist deep in soapy water washing the dinner dishes? The great news is that you can set aside and devote all things to your Heavenly Father! Give God your time, your heart, and your everything!

MARCH 5TH WHAT'S YOUR RUNATUDE?

To be made new in the attitude of your minds; (Ephesians 4:23 NIV)

Every step you take rocks your body, making each stride feel more painstaking than the last. You literally despise every moment! You cannot wait for this run to be behind you and your cozy chair before you. But this is not the first time you have felt this way towards running. Quite the contrary, every time you even think of running, you are overcome by a sense of dread and despair.

Life is much the same way. Anytime you pessimistically face a situation, you will probably end up enduring it much the same way! Is your attitude one that demonstrates hopeless defeat before you even get started? Is it time to give your attitude to God and ask Him to show you how to see things differently? Ask God how to change your view! Don't just run with a smile; embrace an attitude that is God pleasing!

MARCH 6TH RUNNING IS A GAME CHANGER

For I am convinced that neither death nor life, neither angels nor demons, neither the present nor the future, nor any powers, neither height nor depth, nor anything else in all creation, will be able to separate us from the love of God that is in Christ Jesus our Lord. (Romans 8:38-39 NIV)

From a self proclaimed couch potato to a legitimate runner is a life changing event! Once you start running you become a different person. You are a Runner! You are strong, determined, focused, and hard-working. You are a happier and healthier version of you! Instead of dreading your workout, you excitedly and joyously head out on your daily run. The best part is the more you run the more the desire to run overflows inside you. No one can take away all of your effort and hard work.

As a born again child of God, the gift of salvation cannot be taken from you. Jesus is your hope and your promise and nothing can separate you from God and His everlasting love! You are a new creation that is excited by the love and joy of The One who saved you! Today don't run just as a runner but as a runner who is covered by the redeeming blood of Jesus!

MARCH 7TH ROUTINE RUNNING

But if from there you seek the LORD your God, you will find him if you seek him with all your heart and with all your soul. (Deuteronomy 4:29 NIV)

Runners are characters of habit: late night runners who carefully tread through the dark, early morning pace setters who set the mood for a glorious day, and mid afternoon joggers who break up the monotony of an otherwise tedious day. What does your running routine look like? Running the same time of day, every day, just feels right. Natural!

Keeping to a routine schedule for your presence with God can be a great way to ensure you make time. Starting your day in God's peaceful presence or ending it praising His goodness, is a practical way to keep you on track! Plan your times and eagerly meet with your Heavenly Father!

MARCH 8TH RUNNING ENSEMBLE

"There you saw how the LORD your God carried you, as a father carries his son, all the way you went until you reached this place." (Deuteronomy 1:31b NIV)

You put this here, tuck that there, and stuff that in there. You expertly position your water bottles around your hips, hide your keys in your pocket, and place your ear buds in your ears. Finding a perfect place to put your belongings when you run can prove quite a challenge! There can be so much to carry on your run. Carrying all that you need can sometimes make the runner feel more like a pack mule than a training athlete!

Where do you put the heavy things on your heart and mind? Do you bring them to God and lay them down at His feet or do you carry them around all day, heaving the crushing weight on your back? It can be difficult to let go. But when we give God our sorrows and heartaches, that's when we see the goodness of God's grace and mercy abound!

MARCH 9TH I GIVE UP!

For the Spirit God gave us does not make us timid, but gives us power, love and self-discipline. (2 Timothy 1:7 NIV)

You heavily pitch your shoes into the closet. You are never running again. Never ever! You don't even want to see your running shoes again. We probably all have wanted to throw in the towel at one time or another. Running is tough. If it was easy, everyone would do it. But look where you are, look how far you have come! You are improving every day. You can do this!

Today is the day of encouragement in both your running and in your Christian walk. So often we do not see any difference in ourselves so we just want to give up! We feel overwhelmed by the troubles and trials that lie in wait. We trip. We stumble. We fall. But it is not about the challenge or mountain you are facing, it is with Whom you are facing it with. Our God Almighty is with you, He is always there. With God, you can do anything!

MARCH 10TH ROCKING AND RUNNING ABS

All Scripture is God-breathed and is useful for teaching, rebuking, correcting and training in righteousness, so that the servant of God may be thoroughly equipped for every good work. (2 Timothy 3:16-17 NIV)

One, two, three, four, five, six, seven, eight, nine, and ten! Whew! Working your abs is never easy but having a strong core is beneficial for any exercise, especially running! Even though we know core strength is important we so often overlook its benefits!

Just like undervaluing the power of core muscles, we underestimate the power of Scripture! We so often skip essential time digging in and discovering who God is by studying His Word. We miss building a strong spiritual core! So instead of missing the hearty meat and potatoes of God's Word, spend time digesting Scripture! That way when the devil comes your way with his kicks and punches; you will have an arsenal of weaponry ready on your lips and tied to your heart!

MARCH 11TH RUNNERS OF MEN

"Come, follow me," Jesus said, "and I will send you out to fish for people." (Matthew 4:19 NIV)

You are a runner. And a great one at that! So why not be a runner of men? A what? A runner who uses their running platform, exceptional ability, and special talent to invite and tell others about The One to which you run!

Jesus called Peter and Andrew right from the middle of fishing and invited them to continue being fishermen but this time with a twist. They were no longer catching just fish but people! Jesus called them to share the gospel with anyone and everyone. Jesus is calling you from right where you stand, from the sidewalk, treadmill, greenway, or trail you run on! God is, right now, inviting you to be a worker in His kingdom! Glorifying God with everything you are and telling others about the free gift of salvation that only comes through His Son. Run for God's Namesake!

MARCH 12ᵀᴴ RUNNING FEARLESSLY

So then, banish anxiety from your heart and cast off the troubles of your body, (Ecclesiastes 11:10a NIV)

Have you been waiting to start running? Maybe you have convinced yourself that running is just too had to do, too tough. Perhaps you have been running but have been too timid to register for that race you have circled on your calendar. Fears and worries can over take us if we let them!

Today is the day to say no to fear and yes to trusting Jesus! In every area of our lives! Live and run fearlessly today! You can do it! Believe in yourself! There is nothing standing in your way! God will grant you the strength. You just need to be the willing shoes! Run fearlessly and live life fearless today!

MARCH 13ᵀᴴ RUNNING REQUIRES DEDICATION

To this you were called, because Christ suffered for you, leaving you an example, that you should follow in his steps. (1 Peter 2:21 NIV)

What's the recipe behind any runner?

Dedication; and a mighty heaping dose of it!

The running formula for a committed runner requires multiple drops of sweat (literally), hard core courage (absolutely), and the occasional tear (possibly). Runners are all in. They have to be. Running forces the runner to spend time not only on their feet but ample time researching, running, recovering, learning, training, sharing, and planning for their next race.

Following Jesus takes complete, total, and radical devotion and dedication. We must be all hands on deck; hearts open and ready to do the will of our Father.

Jesus requires a wholehearted commitment. Falling in love with Jesus is a task we must daily partake; the run you are eager to run each and every day.

MARCH 14TH BACK ON TRACK

I sought the LORD, and he answered me; he delivered me from all my fears. Those who look to him are radiant; their faces are never covered with shame. (Psalm 34:4-5 NIV)

Shake out those hands! Exhale some air! Push past those feelings that are steadily overwhelming you! Sometimes while running, we need a moment to shake it off and re-focus. Collecting yourself might mean increasing your pace to wake up and gain motivation or maybe slowing down to catch your breath.

In life, we also need moments to refocus. In the business of our lives we can lose sight of what is really important. It can be so easy to just get caught up in living life. Today take a moment to refocus on what is important, Jesus! When you find yourself most stressed and most strained, take a moment and pray. Listen, praise, and give glory to God! Open God's Word and your heart, be attentive to His voice. It is during these moments of quiet that you can find clarity and God can help you get back on track!

MARCH 15TH RUNNERS KNOW BETTER

Whatever you have learned or received or heard from me, or seen in me- put it into practice. And the God of peace will be with you. (Philippians 4:9 NIV)

Do runners know more about training than what we actually put into practice? Uh oh, moment of truth! Take a moment to consider this, in order to run our best it is important to eat and train properly. That being said, we still find ourselves passing up fruits, veggies, and proteins to indulge our sweet tooth on any sugary snack within reach. We also at times pass up the tough training schedule and rely on an old familiar one.

As Christians, we often run into the same pit. We listen to excellent teachings on sermons and podcasts, yet somewhere between hearing and actually doing, we fall between the cracks. We hear, but that's where it stops. So today, make a decision to do more than just absorb God's Word, put those words into practice! Don't walk but run with the good news!

MARCH 16TH RUNNING IN PLACE

"For where your treasure is, there your heart will be also." (Luke 12:34 NIV)

Getting nowhere? Feel like you are forever running in place? You most certainly are if you are running on a treadmill! Treadmills not only offer a great workout but are convenient on those freezing cold, deep snow, or rainy days. Treadmills are easy to jump on and get your work out done, especially when it's conveniently waiting for you in your living room.

Perhaps you feel as if you are stuck on a treadmill, running in place in your faith. Not seeing any real heart changes, growth, or maturity? The question you have to ask is; where are you? Where is your heart, your passion? Do you live to glorify God and serve Him with every piece of your being? Are you diligently seeking to know your Creator? Do you put God first? Are there things, people, or areas in your life that are taking the top shelf above God? It's time to jump off the treadmill and triumphantly start running down the path that leads towards Jesus!

MARCH 17ᵀᴴ GOD'S RUNNING WITH ME

I will fear no evil, for you are with me; your rod and staff, they comfort me. (Psalm 23:4b NIV)

So often it can feel like we are running the race of our lives alone. Solo. We get easily tired, utterly exhausted, and completely worn out both body and soul. The great news is that when we become drained by the strains of this world, we can turn to God. We can come, just as we are, achy and dirty, with smelly sneakers included. God knows what you are up against. The obstacles you have had to rush over. The bumps and bruises, the sprains and strains you have incurred along the way.

You are never running alone. God is with you always, every day, 24/7, rain or shine. So today remember that God is with you every step of the way! God wants every piece and every part of you. God loves you, cares for you, and has a perfect plan for you! Trust the King of kings.

MARCH 18ᵀᴴ RUNNING CRUSHED

For we are God's handiwork, created in Christ Jesus to do good works, which God prepared in advance for us to do. (Ephesians 2:10 NIV)

Your dreams are crushed. You feel utterly defeated. Feeling like a failure can come easily for dreamers like runners. Runners place high and sometimes even unrealistic expectations on our shoulders. If we do not meet them, we feel utterly defeated.

In life, feeling unsuccessful often plays a familiar tune in our head. We feel as though we have failed in our jobs, failed as a student, failed in relationships, or failed as a Christ follower. When you feel overwhelming feelings of disappointment, it is important to settle one thing right out of the gate. You are not a failure! Not even close! God loves you and has a plan for you and your life. When you start to feel this way, it is important to bring these feelings and insecurities to God. The Lord's mercies are overflowing!

MARCH 19TH RUNNING FROM YOUR KNEES

"I have been crucified with Christ and I no longer live, but Christ lives in me. The life I now live in the body, I live by faith in the Son of God, who loved me and gave himself for me." (Galatians 2:20 NIV)

There are a lot of "sayings" that don't make a whole lot of sense, such as… "She ran as fast as lightening" or "He runs all the time". No one is obviously as speedy as lightening and no one can consistently run all day and all night, day in and day out! Even if we wanted to! So how can you possibly run on your knees? It is from your knees that we as Christian runners need to learn to do everything in life!

We learn how to live in complete submission to our Heavenly Father. We learn to surrender ourselves and our attitudes to God and live our lives with Him in total control. This is easier said than done! We want to "run" our own lives. We want to have the last say! But it is not until we learn to be in complete submission to God that we receive the true gift of joy and peace that comes from being a child of God and submitting to His will!

MARCH 20TH RUNNING REDO

"The thief comes only to steal and kill and destroy; I have come that they may have life, and have it to the full." (John 10:10 NIV)

Need a do over? Feel like you would give anything just for a second chance to do it better, to run it again. You are convinced that if you were granted a redo you would have shaved off those precious seconds. You are kicking yourself for not training harder, running faster, and for not giving it your all.

Ever feel this way in life? If only you could have taken back that mean word you said, spent more time with your family, or shown a little more patience and kindness to a friend. Although we cannot travel back in time and do it differently, we do have the power to change the here and now in a way that glorifies God! We are not perfect, not by a long shot! However, we serve a perfect Savior, a Savior who was the perfect sacrifice for our sins. Through Christ's death and resurrection, we can live life and have it to the full. So maybe we cannot run that race again, we can run forward having the freedom to run in a way that glorifies our perfect King! So run onward, not looking behind, but joyfully surging confidently ahead by God's grace and mercy!

MARCH 21ST RUN LIKE SOMEONE IS WATCHING

Jesus knew what they were thinking and asked, "Why are you thinking these things in your hearts?" (Luke 5:22 NIV)

You kick it in. All runners do. The moment we know someone is watching us run, our heart skips a beat and our feet start flying. It is easy to put on a good show while someone is looking and then take a breather once you turn the corner! Just as your running transforms when someone else is observing, have you ever acted differently when you are around your pastor?

Perhaps you act one way at work and then present yourself in a completely different way at church or in the living room of your Bible study. How would your attitude change if Jesus was your fellow co-worker, a passerby on the street, or the clerk behind the counter? We never really stop to think that our King not only sees everything we do, and hears everything we say, but even knows our thoughts! Challenge yourself to be positive in every situation and see others for who they are, wonderful children of God. Let love and mercy flow out of your heart and show grace towards others. Run and live your life in a way that glorifies God, even when you think no one is watching!

MARCH 22ND RUNNING AS EASY AS PIE

Dear friends, do not be surprised at the fiery ordeal that has come on you to test you, as though something strange were happening to you. (1 Peter 4:12 NIV)

You've seen them. The people that make running look effortless! They enthusiastically fly by, easily breathing, with no signs of strain or effort evident on their carefree face. They make running look like a breeze. Running beside this confident runner can be discouraging as you struggle with every stride you take. Just keep in mind, everyone has struggles in their lives, everyone!

Our Christian walk can feel much the same way. For some followers it appears as if they do not struggle a day in their life. They just seem to have it all together, neat and tidy, with everything in perfect order, and in place. But if we took the time to look into their lives, it would show anything but an orderly and perfect life. The only difference is they know who to cast their cares on. We all go through trials and struggles. No one is exempt! We are all going through ups and downs in life but by God's grace we can find peace, love, and joy no matter what! If you find everything in your life going your way, thank God for it. If you are struggling, thank God for His faithfulness. Keep praying, trusting God, and running forward!

MARCH 23RD MIND OVER RUNNING

Set your minds on things above, not on earthly things. (Colossians 3:2 NIV)
Squish, squash, squish, squash! Your feet sing as they methodically hit the water trenched pavement. As you run through a steady dose of rain against your skin, where do your thoughts travel? Do you wish you never started your run today, longing for it to be over? Or do you thank God for the rain that nourishes His creation and helps the beauty of nature blossom and bloom?

Like all thoughts in life, we can choose our mindset. We can focus on thoughts that are holy, loving, and godly or we can brood on worries, fears, and thoughts that cripple our hearts, minds, and feet. When we run, we run in such a way that sets our goals and aspirations beyond the finish line. As we pound away the miles, runners learn to push past thoughts that consume our minds with failure and instead concentrate on dreams that inspire. In the same way, when we live, let our minds be filled with things that glorify our Father in heaven! Let us cast out every thought that displeases God and set our hearts and mind on things above!

MARCH 24TH JUST KEEP RUNNING!

The LORD is my light and my salvation—whom I shall I fear? The LORD is the stronghold of my life—of whom shall I be afraid? (Psalm 27:1 NIV)
"Just one more step, just one more!"

You patiently assure yourself as you repeat the phrase again and again. Running at this point feels like the most unnatural thing on earth. Excruciating! Overwhelming! Impossible! You literally feel like if you stop, even for one moment, you might never run again.

Life can feel much the same way. Work, bills, people, and tasks enclose around us. Choking us! Fear, anxiety, and doubt overwhelm us as we continue trudging along. It is at this point we have to make a crucial decision. We can either (A) continue sinking through the muck and the mire or (B) give God the issues that are making every step of our lives seem unbearable and impossible. We can depend on God's strength and His strength alone. So it is no longer us keeping step but us relying on God's timing. And God's timing is always perfect! Just keep running, just keep running with God!

MARCH 25ᵀᴴ RUNNING THE ROAD

Trust in the LORD with all your heart and lean not on your own understanding; in all your ways submit to him, and he will make your paths straight. (Proverbs 3:5-6 NIV)

It's a surprise! Today's run, tomorrow's run, and every future run. You never know what you will encounter, what obstacle you might hit, or who you might meet along the way. Of course you know where those daunting hills lie in wait and where the easy, scenic portion of your run peacefully awaits, but everything else in between... That's all open game!

Just like running an unknown road, you never know what surprise will show up in our lives. Sure we expect to eat breakfast, go to work, have lunch, make dinner, do laundry, and help the kids with homework, but life is more than just the tasks that we do and the places we need to be. Whatever else shows up in your life day to day, good or bad, God will always be there with open arms to carry you through. When we lean on God and seek Him every step we take, we can be assured of one thing, we can trust Him every step of the way. God loves you. Trust Him. Rely on God each and every day, leaning on the promise that His way is the path to everlasting life.

MARCH 26ᵀᴴ CHILDLIKE RUNNING

See what great love the Father has lavished on us, that we should be called children of God! And that is what we are! (1 John 3:1a NIV)

They run here. They run there. They playfully run circles around you. Literally! By the time you put your shoes on they have easily run the driveway. Not once but twice! They are not even out of breath. Not even a little! Ah, to run like a child! But as we mature our lives change. We have jobs, families, and friends who count on us. Depend on us.

But wouldn't it be nice to tap into that inner child sometime, even if it's just on your run? Children run this way because they know their parents love them; they are carefree and seem amazed at everything. They know their parents will take care of them. The way children count on their earthly parents' provision, is an example of how we can depend on our Heavenly Father. God's love is greater than any love we could ever fathom. God has a perfect plan for you and your life. So that you, like a child, can run freely in the loving backyard of our Heavenly Father.

MARCH 27ᵀᴴ LIGHTING YOUR PATH

Your word is a lamp for my feet, a light on my path. (Psalm 119:105 NIV)

Evening swoops in around you. In the middle of your run, darkness starts to drop a canopy over you, drastically narrowing your vision. You begin to worry. At this rate you will end up making it home in the pitch black, unable to see anything in front of you. You start to feel a little uneasy. Then all of a sudden the luminescence of the automatic street lamps brightens the once dark path. You release a sigh of relief! There's no denying that running down a well lit trail makes things much easier. The same applies for living life in a dark and dreary world.

The awesome news is that God's Word lights our path! Our Heavenly Father's love guides our willing hands and feet, showing us what to do. God's Word illuminates even the darkest corners of our hearts. When you are feeling in a dark place, switch on the light, adjust your reading glasses, and pick up your Bible. It's probably sitting right there beside you on the coffee table. Read and ask God what He would have you do. Where God would have you go! Our Creator did not leave us all alone on this earth. God gave us the gift of the Holy Spirit residing within us and His Word to illuminate the path for our weary feet!

MARCH 28ᵀᴴ PSALMS RUNNER

Praise the LORD. Praise God in his sanctuary; praise him in his mighty heavens. Praise him for his acts of power; praise him for his surpassing greatness. (Psalm 150:1-2 NIV)

Are you ready to become a Psalms Runner? The Bible was written not just in the delightful times but during times of deep despair and pain. To be a Psalm runner we need to praise God not only during the easy sunshine filled days of running along on a beach, but during the bad, the tough, and the ugly. We all know that is easier said than done! Pray for Jesus to give you a heart that is trusting, yieldable, and moldable in His hands.

Ask God to show you how to lean on Him through both the good and bad and how to put a song of praise in your heart no matter what the circumstances! If you are running on a treadmill this week or cross training on an elliptical machine or stationary bike, write out your favorite Psalm and post it where you can meditate on it while you work out your body! Get moving both body and soul!

MARCH 29TH RUNNING POWERHOUSE

But he said to me, "My grace is sufficient for you, for my power is made perfect in weakness." (2 Corinthians 12:9a NIV)

Flex those glorious muscles! That's right, you've got them for sure! As runners we seek to be strong, not weak! We train hard to build those powerhouse muscles so we can easily conquer those mountainous climbs!

Life closely mimics our need for power. We seek not to be powerless but powerful! We painfully strive to get the upper hand in our jobs, in our relationships, and in our finances, sometimes at a very high cost. So when Paul says,

"For when I am weak, then I am strong."

(2 Corinthians 12:10b NIV)

We begin to scratch our heads. But as Christians, we know our strength is found in God, not in ourselves! The Creator of the universe believes in you and will turn your weakness into strength if you lean on Him! We have an unlimited power source through God! When we stop depending on ourselves and trust in God's power alone, all things become possible!

MARCH 30TH THE ULTIMATE PRICE

But he was pierced for our transgressions, he was crushed for our iniquities; the punishment that brought us peace was on him, and by his wounds we are healed. (Isaiah 53:5 NIV)

Stop running! That's right! Take time today in remembrance of the ultimate price Jesus paid with His blood, through His suffering and death on the cross. From the flogging Jesus received, the twisted crown of thorns pressed down on His beautiful head, to the piercing nails that drove through His life-giving hands and feet, to His final breath he breathed as He hung on the cross. No amount of pain you have ever experienced while running will ever come close to Christ's suffering. Not ever.

Yet Jesus was innocent. Perfect. Jesus chose to take our place. Our place! So no matter what you have done and no matter what you are going through, Jesus knows and understands. Everything! We are never out of range of God's loving grasp and His unmerited forgiveness. So run today in lavish joy and overflowing gratitude that Jesus paid the ultimate sacrifice! How can we be anything less than joyous? Triumphant!

MARCH 31ˢᵀ UNSTOPPABLE RUNNER

If we live, we live for the Lord; and if we die, we die for the Lord. So, whether we live or die, we belong to the Lord. (Romans 14:8 NIV)

Nothing is going to stop you! You are all in! You are running with all your might and with everything you are! Nothing and no one can stand in your way! With every step and every stride you exude confidence and determination!

When you place our faith in Christ, go all in. Place all your hope in Jesus and perfectly rest in His peaceful embrace. No obstacle can stand in your way because our faith is in God and you know that He is with you every step of the way. Live a life that is all in for Jesus today. In everything you do and in everything you say point others to the hope and joy you have found in Christ!

"The kingdom of heaven is like treasure hidden in a field. When a man found it, he hid it again, and then in his joy went and sold all he had and bought that field." (Matthew 13:44 NIV)

APRIL 1ˢᵀ VICTORY LAP!

Jesus said to her, "I am the resurrection and the life. The one who believes in me will live, even though they die; and whoever lives by believing in me will never die. Do you believe this?" (John 11:25-26 NIV)

Feeling victorious? You should, because all believers have triumph in Jesus!

"But thanks be to God! He gives us the victory through our Lord Jesus Christ." (1 Corinthians 15:57 NIV)

We live because Christ lives! Run in appreciative victory today! Give God the praise, the glory, and the honor He forever deserves! We are triumphant in Christ!

The tomb is empty and Jesus has risen!

"He is not the God of the dead, but of the living!" (Mark 12:27a NIV)

APRIL 2ᴺᴰ RUNNING IN THE RAIN

"You heavens above, rain down my righteousness; let the clouds shower it down. Let the earth open wide, let salvation spring up, let righteousness flourish with it; I, the LORD, have created it." (Isaiah 45:8 NIV)

Rain heavily falls down on your head, wildly dripping into your eyes, and dampening everything that you once dryly wore. Your shoes crash heavily into water puddles as your feet begin to make a sloshing thud against the wet pavement. Running in the rain can be either one of two experiences: one that makes you feel like a child excitedly dodging puddles or one where you solely focus on a very dreary, muddy, and damp situation!

Instead of dwelling on the rains stickiness, fixate on the goodness of God and the many blessings He currently is and will pour down on you. God loves you so much! More than you could ever imagine. Take a minute while running today to count all those blessings. Those blessings will quickly start to outnumber the glistening rain drops. So even if you are having a miserable day, you have a choice to turn your perspective into one that is pleasing to your Father. Let your perspective be an attitude that generously rains down love and kindness!

APRIL 3ᴿᴰ PRAY. THEN RUN

Devote yourselves to prayer, being watchful and thankful. (Colossians 4:2 NIV)

A sense of anxiety and excitement heavily hangs in the air. You recognize the scene. It's the final countdown before the race and every runner is doing their pre-run routine. Some runners hurriedly dodge to the bathroom, some warm up, while others can be seen stretching and excitedly chatting to one another.

We all have a pre-race routine; however there might be something very important you are forgetting. Prayer. Give your run to God and ask that through your run, you would bring glory to Him. Ask that God would use this time to draw you closer to Him. Pray that you would discover more about God and His love. Pray that you would see those you pass as God Almighty sees them, with His love and grace. Devote your run to God and pray that you would point others to Him! Pray before each and everything you do! Ask, and then move. Pray then run!

APRIL 4ᵀᴴ RUNNING INTO A NEW YOU

Therefore, if anyone is in Christ, the new creation has come: The old has gone, the new is here! (2 Corinthians 5:17 NIV)

When you became a runner, you changed! You made the decision to embark on an adventure that left your old self behind on the couch, and began a new voyage that challenged yourself both mentally and physically. You became a more disciplined, healthier, and a more focused version of you. Your favorite jeans feel looser, your energy spikes, and your attitude changes! Not only can you feel the difference, you can see the difference!

When you become a Christian you become a new person in Christ. The old is gone! You are transformed, seeking to be more and more like The One who saved you! Your words change. Your actions change. Your thoughts change. The life you once lived that focused on pleasing yourself, is now seeking to live a life that brings glory and honor to our Heavenly Father! Live as the newer, healthier, better you!

APRIL 5ᵀᴴ A SKIP IN YOUR STEP

A cheerful heart is good medicine, but a crushed spirit dries up the bones. (Proverbs 17:22 NIV)

Wait for it. Wait for it. Okay, there it is! Your smile, there it is! It's time to run in a way that's not so serious. Train hard (of course!), stick to your training (please!), and give it your all (most definitely!), but also leave a little room in your run for a laugh, chuckle, and a smile. Diligently train but remember to enjoy yourself!

So turn that frown upside down and laugh a little. God loves you! You are God's chosen child!

Life can leave us unsmiling. Bills need to be paid, work needs to be done, and projects have deadlines. But remember to find joy in God and in what He has given you to do. Live with the everlasting joy that can only come through life in Jesus Christ. Joy in your family. Joy in your job. Joy in your run. Joy even in the hardships. Yes that's right joy even in hardships! So run today with the everlasting joy of Jesus in your heart. Crack a joke. Giggle a little. Giggle a lot! You are worth it! Your smile and your positive attitude can be a light that points others to Jesus! Let your love and joy in Christ be contagious!

APRIL 6ᵀᴴ A RUNNING TAKE OVER

So that you may live a life worthy of the Lord and please him in every way: bearing fruit in every good work, growing in the knowledge of God, (Colossians 1:10 NIV)

Admit it! Running has you hook, line, and sinker! You love running and cannot wait until you get the chance to put your shoes on again! At first, you approached running apprehensively. You ran just once or twice a week, that was it! But, as with most runners' experience, the more you run, the more running has won you over!

When we accept Jesus as our Lord and Savior, it can be easy not to know what to expect! At first we assume we will give God our Sundays and then in turn He will give us salvation, peace, joy, love, and the rest of our week. Of course these are all great gifts but we forget one very important thing! Jesus wants all of you!

Every day and every second! God desires to use you in every area, every situation, and use every personal interaction in your life to His glory. So pitch the training program that only has God penciled in on Sundays and run with Him every moment of every day!

APRIL 7ᵀᴴ COMPASSIONATE RUNNERS

"The King will reply, 'Truly I tell you, whatever you did for one of the least of these brothers and sisters of mine, you did for me.'" (Matthew 25:40 NIV)

Let's run together to help someone else! Races and friendly runs that raise money for various organizations and causes are held around the country throughout the year. It is time to put your running skills to good use! Choose to run, raise money, and elevate awareness for others in need! If you are unable to run, there are always races and events that need help volunteering! Kindly giving of yourself and your time is a great way to be Christ's hands and feet. To show God's love for others in the things that you say and the things that you do can make all the difference in someone else's life.

Often the best way to show Christ to someone is to show them Christ living in you! Boldly live your proclamation of your Christian faith by the giving of your love, abilities, and time! So how can you make a difference today in the life of someone else? How can you show others the love of Jesus that wells inside of you? Today pray for God to show you a way to show the love of Christ for all to see!

APRIL 8ᵀᴴ RUNNERS JUST GET IT!

But you are a chosen people, a royal priesthood, a holy nation, God's special possession, that you may declare the praises of him who called you out of darkness into his wonderful light. (1 Peter 2:9 NIV)

Jaws drop! Eyes roll. They stare at you in utter amazement! People that don't run cannot in their wildest dreams understand why you would want to run countless miles of turmoil day in and day out!

Following Jesus can look just as confusing to those on the outside. Jesus calls us to live a life that is totally crazy compared to how the world tells us to live! Jesus showed us to humble ourselves and be a servant. The world tells us that we are number one! Jesus taught us to have a heart that freely gives. The world encourages us to build up our own bank accounts! The world promotes that there are many ways to get to heaven. Christ's teaching is completely opposite from the world view! So even though we might be misunderstood, we can stand strong and find confidence to live for God, through Him who gives us strength!

APRIL 9TH DISCOURAGED RUNNER

May the God of hope fill you with all joy and peace as you trust in him, so that you may overflow with hope by the power of the Holy Spirit. (Romans 15:13 NIV)

Feeling let down? You did everything you were supposed to do! You faithfully rest, stretch, massage, stay hydrated, eat healthy, and do your best to find the best pair of shoes for your feet. You do anything and everything to stay healthy and then disaster strikes! You keep getting injured!

Sound familiar in life? Perhaps you feel like you live a life that glorifies God and because of that you feel entitled to that promotion or to buy that car you always wanted. But that is where we have it all wrong! God and only God knows what is best for you! Not you, but God! Our Creator promises to provide all that we need. So when we think we deserve more or should have gotten our way, we are then dealing with what we want and what we think we need, instead of what God has in store for us. Turn your discouragement into gratitude! Change your grumblings into praises! You are His and everything that you have is a gift from God!

APRIL 10TH CROSS TRAINING

Praise be to the LORD my Rock, who trains my hands for war, my fingers for battle. Psalm 144:1 (NIV)

Pedal it, swim it, climb it, hike it, kick it, jump it, roll it, swing it, punch it, stretch it, and push it. Cross training offers so many amazing benefits to the runner! So dive in a pool, jump on your bike, strap on some skis, play a game of soccer or tennis, or grab a paddle and ride in a kayak or on a paddleboard.

Cross training is not unique to running but to your faith walk as well! There are so many ways to train in your faith, like; reading your Bible, listening to God's Word audibly or hearing a sermon online, joining or starting a Bible group, getting involved in your church, going out into your community, or going out into your world on mission trips! Find new and exciting ways to grow your faith and challenge yourself in your relationship with God. There are endless possibilities at your fingertips!

APRIL 11ᵀᴴ JUST SAY YES!

"Here I am! I stand at the door and knock. If anyone hears my voice and opens the door, I will come in and eat with that person, and they with me." (Revelation 3:20 NIV)

That's right, say yes! Wave those hands and dance like you just don't care! It's time to say yes to running! Yes to change! Yes to your biggest goals! Yes to the new you and who you want to be! Kick down and charge past all those excuses and obstacles that have continued to stand in your way! So what's holding you on the sidelines? What's holding you back from achieving your dreams in running?

What's stopping you from starting the race leading to eternal life? Before we become Christians we are all sidelined, lost within this dark world. Choosing Jesus Christ as our Lord and Savior is just that, a personal choice. We have to choose to accept Jesus. We are not saved by just going to church every Sunday or because we are a good person. It is only through faith in Jesus that we are able to be with God eternally in heaven. Jesus is calling us to open that door and invite Him in! Run and pull open the door; God is calling your name!

APRIL 12ᵀᴴ GLOBAL RUNNERS

May the peoples praise you, God; may all the peoples praise you. May the nations be glad and sing for joy, for you rule the peoples with equity and guide the nations of the earth. (Psalm 67:3-4 NIV)

You can find them trotting through the desert and skipping through the sand. You will spot them sprinting over mountaintops and scampering through the forest. You can even identify them trudging through the snow and sweating under a scorching sun. Across the globe runners may look different and speak uniquely but they all run!

Jesus followers might worship differently, they might sing differently, and they might even pray differently but they all have one thing in common…their love for Jesus. We might all praise the one true King but how we live out our lives, as Christian's, vary greatly.

In many countries to follow Jesus is illegal and downright dangerous. If you are living in a place where Jesus is openly glorified and praised, thank Him, and remember to always aggressively pray for your brothers and sisters around the world who are being persecuted because the follow Christ. Pray for the courage and strength to live for God today! He gives them the courage.

APRIL 13TH MODEL RUNNER

Join together in following my example, brothers and sisters, and just as you have us as a model, keep your eyes on those who live as we do. (Philippians 3:17 NIV)

Wow look at them run! What an inspiration! Is there an impressive runner that you wish to emulate? You are encouraged by their hard work, the difficult obstacles they have had to overcome, or by the sheer number of their wins? Because of their endless drive, you carefully watch how they train, what they eat, and the type of running shoes they wear. You hope to run just like them!

Human motivation comes in all sizes, ages, and races. Inspiration in our faith walk is no different! Paul encourages us to take note of others who live a life in total submission and humility to Christ. A Christian who lives their lives to glorify God in all they say and do! Who in your life inspires you to deepen your relationship with Jesus? Maybe your mom, dad, teacher, pastor, neighbor, or a grandparent lives a life that encourages you! Live in a way that points others to Christ! Live your life on fire for Christ! Just as important as it is to see a Christ like example is to be an example!

APRIL 14TH RUNNING WITH SOME OOMPH!

Jesus answered, "It is written: 'Man shall not live on bread alone, but on every word that comes from the mouth of God.' " (Matthew 4:4 NIV)

Needing a boost of power? Open your Bible, select a verse, and commit that scripture to memory. Then when you are in need of a serious source of encouragement and strength you have your secret weapon waiting and ready to go!

Hiding God's Word deep in your heart gives you an instant shield when the devil comes against you with his fiery arrows! God's Word is a source of inspiration at our fingertips. When we fill our hearts and minds with God's love and strength we can overcome anything that comes our way! So run with God's Word planted deep within your hearts and minds. Always have it ready on the tip of your tongue. Use God's Word not only to kindle a fire inside of you but ignite those who run alongside you both on the road and in life.

APRIL 15TH TIME, MONEY, AND RUNNING

Keep your lives free from the love of money and be content with what you have, because God said, "Never will I leave you; never will I forsake you." (Hebrews 13:5 NIV)

At first glance, running appears pretty cheap. All you need are your feet... right? But when you take a closer look into your bank account, the numbers reveal otherwise! You have to buy new shoes every so many miles, don sweat wicking, non chaffing clothing, a running watch, pay registration fees, hotel, and travel fees for races, and buy healthy foods and drinks that power your nutrition. Somehow running went from a simple foot race to some serious funds being kept from your savings!

Finances and what we do with our money is important to God. Money is mentioned again and again in God's Word. Where are you spending the resources God has given you? Where you put your money shows what is important to you! Find a cause or charity that is near and dear to your heart and support it. God has blessed you with so much. Find ways, no matter how big or small, to bless others out of the abundance God has blessed you!

APRIL 16TH PEACEFUL RUNNING

Now may the Lord of peace himself give you peace at all times and in every way. The Lord be with all of you. (2 Thessalonians 3:16 NIV)

Your shoes heavily pound the ground. Every step seems to rock your entire body. You ache. Everywhere! You are grossly sweaty, steaming hot, and unbearably tired. Every stride feels far from peaceful! Finding tranquility while running seems almost laughable but then again maybe not.

In life we often try to tiredly trudge through the mud, muck, and mire completely by our self. We forget that we do not have to run the story of our lives all alone. We serve a God who offers us hope and peace even in the middle of life's craziest moments. Even when our world seems to be swirling around us, God is our center, the focal point to which we cling. Our God is a God of peace. Our Heavenly Father wants us to lean our heavy, sweaty bodies against Him with each and every achy step we take. God wants our all, our everything! Contently run down the path with our hearts and minds leaning on the Almighty who gives us strength! Only in God can we find perfect peace!

APRIL 17TH IF YOU CAN DREAM IT, YOU CAN RUN IT!

Now to him who is able to do immeasurably more than all we ask or imagine, according to his power that is at work within us, (Ephesians 3:20 NIV)

Close your eyes and ponder. What do you dream of doing? Do you see yourself quietly pattering along a tranquil trail under the shadiness of a tree lined canopy? Or maybe your aspirations take you to not just completing but winning a race? Perhaps your hopes are set on finishing your very first marathon or even an ultra?

We all treasure dreams. Find hope in your beautiful ambitions. What are your aspirations? Where do you feel God calling and leading you? Is God leading you to accomplish something even beyond your wildest dreams! You can do it! Believe in yourself because God believes in you!

APRIL 18ᵀᴴ RUNNING FEELS IMPOSSIBLE

Jesus looked at them and said, "With man this is impossible, but with God all things are possible." (Matthew 19:26 NIV)

You feel defeated! Utterly conquered! How will you ever be able to run that far, that fast! As if you cannot possibly go the distance, maintain the pace, or finish the race? In running it can be easy to feel overwhelmed and convince yourself that running is just out of your league.

Are you facing a situation right now that feels impossible? As if you are in over your head and your worries are steadily rising? We can feel overwhelmed in our roles as a husband, wife, mom, dad, sister, brother, or child, as well as within our roles at home, school, work, or church. We serve a God through which all things are possible! God has created you stronger, smarter, and more talented than you can ever imagine. You can do more than you ever dreamed of! Keep pushing and breaking down the walls that stand in your way! Rely on God in every situation and circumstance that seems too big to take on all alone. Our King is all powerful, all knowing, and nothing is out of His control.

APRIL 19ᵀᴴ RUNNING IN THE QUIET

Yes, my soul, find rest in God; my hope comes from him." (Psalm 62:5 NIV)

It's perfectly still. If it were not for the steady flow of your breath, it would be completely quiet. A refreshing sense of peace and solitude envelope you. But that's why you run here, in the middle of these serene woods, on this soft wooded trail. You are seeking tranquility and serenity after a long day's work. You purposefully avoid the busy hub at the gym and you specifically picked this path to avoid any and all traffic.

God is our perfect peace. The Lord is the soothing balm for our unsettled soul. Like the placid trail before you, you can find comfort in God's presence. His are the open and inviting arms we can always turn to. So turn off and unplug the clamorous distractions around you and turn to the peace of God's loving presence!

APRIL 20TH A RUNNER'S HOLD UP

He has shown you, O mortal, what is good. And what does the LORD require of you? To act justly and to love mercy and to walk humbly with your God. (Micah 6:8 NIV)

What is the only thing that can stop a runner in his or her tracks? You guessed it… an injury! Injuries grab our attention and fast! Injuries pluck us from the trodden path and immediately to the couch in a heartbeat. You cannot ignore pain!

In our everyday life it might not be an injury but any number of things that force us to our knees. We become so focused on our lives, our jobs, and on our families, that we forget about God. We tend to go about our day without giving God even a second glance or a passing thought. But God in His love and mercy cares about you! God just doesn't want some of you, He wants all of you! So it might take an injury, an illness, a heartache, a hang-up, a break up, or a setback to focus our hearts and minds on God! For it is wiser to take one crippled step in God's direction than a thousand strides going the wrong way!

APRIL 21ST ZEALOUS RUNNING

Never be lacking in zeal, but keep your spiritual fervor, serving the Lord. (Romans 12:11 NIV)

Running requires us to be zealous, forever seeking to be a better, faster, and a more efficient runner. Runners eagerly wake up to run, eat to run, and plan their day around their run. But does your passion for Christ exceed your fervor for running?

Are you earnestly seeking to live a life that brings glory and honor to your Lord and Savior? Are you giving God your every breath, your every passion, and your very reason for living? Are you intensely running to Jesus with all of your heart? God wants the top spot in our lives, not just falling somewhere between the other desires of our hearts.

Imagine sprinting for that sweet prize of deserved recognition for all of your hard work. The one holding that precious prize is God. Run towards God, with every ounce of your being, to hear Him reward you with those sweet words…

"Well done, good and faithful servant!" See (Matthew 25:23 NIV)

APRIL 22ND FALLING HARD

But when he saw the wind, he was afraid and, beginning to sink, cried out, "Lord, save me!" Immediately Jesus reached out his hand and caught him. "You of little faith," he said, "why did you doubt?" (Matthew 14:30-31 NIV)

"Ah! Ow! Ouch!" You anxiously yelp as you fall to the hard ground. You gingerly rub your knees as you pick yourself up. It can be easy to trip and fall, especially when you are tired or find yourself heading down a path brimming with thistles, branches, sticks, stones, and uneven ground. It can also become troublesome to navigate your way along a path when running at night or under dimly lit streetlamps.

Our chances of falling in life also seem to increase during the same conditions they did while running. We are more likely to worry or fall into temptation, sin, or trouble when we are tired, when our path is full of unforeseen and cumbersome obstacles and challenges, or when we cannot clearly see our path. We often descend quickly when we cannot make our way or struggle through life's brambles and briers. So throw up your hands and reach for Jesus! Only Jesus can save, only He can guide. Only through Jesus can we find the road to everlasting life!

APRIL 23RD RUNNING THROUGH SICKNESS

Who forgives all your sins and heals all your diseases, (Psalm 103:3 NIV)

"Ah-choo!"

You loudly sneeze as you sluggishly wipe your runny nose. You feel exhausted, weak, and completely sapped of energy, as you muster all your efforts in your feeble attempt to jog down the sidewalk. To be sick is bad enough, but to be sick and run can leave you feeling like finishing all those long miles is impossible!

Feeling less than par can make any run incredibly tough, if not impossible!

Are you feeling less than par in your day to day? Are you tired of the hurts and struggles in your life looming over your head? If so give them to God! Your Heavenly Father cares for you and wants to carry you through them into the life of abundance and prosperity He has planned for you. Don't go through life one more second feeling sub-par. Cast all of your cares on God. Only God can make you whole! Stop running through them alone!

APRIL 24TH DON'T JUST TALK ABOUT IT, RUN!

Do not merely listen to the word, and so deceive yourselves. Do what it says. (James 1:22 NIV)

True or False? Running is easier said than done? True, of course! This simple fact divides the game talkers from the diehards. It can be much easier to talk the talk then to actually run the run. Anyone can boast about running a race, but actually going the distance, requires a whole lot more than just empty chatter!

So often we can be like that in our everyday lives. We often rattle on about what we can do for our neighbor or how we can serve in the church, yet we fail to put those fruitful words into action! So put your shoes to the pavement and do what you say! Invite that friend to church. Visit a neighbor in need. Volunteer at a local soup kitchen. Go on a mission trip. Be Christ's hands and feet! Be God's love and smile for all to see!

APRIL 25ᵀᴴ RUNNING ON EMPTY?

Come near to God and he will come near to you.

(James 4:8a NIV)

Craving French fries? Maybe you have a hankering for a humongous bowl of vanilla ice cream dripping with swirly chocolate and caramel? Whatever the guilty food pleasure you are longing for, one thing is probably true; you just finished a run, and you are ravenous! You feel like a car out of gas and you desire to eat anything and everything to fill the empty pit of your stomach.

Like the hollowness of a hungry stomach, do you ever feel like your soul is starving? Are you running low on God? The good news is that when you seek God you will find Him! Unlike the empty calories of the world, our Savior's love, grace, and mercy are sure to fill you up and give you a deep joy that only comes from Him. So leave your fork and spoon in the silverware drawer, grab your Bible and find a comfortable spot alone, and be in the presence of your Savior! Fill your spiritual hunger with Jesus!

APRIL 26ᵀᴴ EYES ON THE PRIZE

Fixing our eyes on Jesus, the pioneer and perfecter of faith. For the joy set before him he endured the cross, scorning its shame, and sat down at the right hand of the throne of God. (Hebrews 12:2 NIV)

Imagine you are running along a beautiful tree lined trail. The sky is a gorgeous blue and the sun is glimmering brightly through the branches. You are contently trotting along, intently looking at your phone, when all of a sudden you fall flat on your face. A rock, unbeknown to you, tripped your left foot as it sat jutted among the forest floor. It can be quite easy to trip and fall while running, especially when you are not paying attention to your surroundings and the trail ahead!

How many times in life do we fall flat on our face? Instead of keeping our eyes straight, focused on our Lord and Savior, we have our attention on anything and everything but Him. So today is the day to take your eyes off the world and glue them to your Savior and King. Where are you fixing your eyes? Jesus is our prize, our hope!

APRIL 27TH THE RUNNER I SEEK TO BECOME

And we boast in the hope of the glory of God. Not only so, but we also glory in our sufferings, because we know that suffering produces perseverance; perseverance, character; and character, hope. (Romans 5:2b-4 NIV)

We strive to be the best! We push ourselves to be the very best runner we can be! We desire to smash our own personal goals and shatter the expectations of others! We train hard, eat smart, and then run again! We are determined!

As a follower of Jesus Christ we run life in a way, that with every step we take, we aim to become more and more like our Messiah. The Christian race is not easy. It is chock-full of trials, temptations, and struggles. We sometimes want to quit. We want to give up. Instead of looking to Christ, we look within ourselves for the power to go on, but our strength is never enough! It is only when we keep our eyes on Jesus and throw up our hands in radical commitment to Jesus Christ that we can discover everlasting joy in Him! God desires us to grow and to mature in faith. To deepen our love and dependence on Him! Give God your very best and your all!

APRIL 28TH TURNING IT AROUND!

"So do not fear, for I am with you; do not be dismayed, for I am your God. I will strengthen and help you; I will uphold you with my righteous right hand." (Isaiah 41:10 NIV)

Feeling like you are running on a spinning top? Feeling discouraged and spun all around? Running has its ups and downs. Some days we feel as if we are having the best run of our lives, racing down a mountaintop with the wind in our hair. While other days, we struggle just to get down the driveway.

Life can feel much the same, full of ups and downs, with downs coming to us in a variety of shape and sizes. Although discouragements can and will happen, what is more important than falling down is Who you depend on to get you back up. Who loves you, Who protects you, and Who is faithful. God! God is our source! God is our fountain of courage and our strength. So even if you feel like you are riding a roller coaster, remember God is with you! God is with you wherever you may go!

APRIL 29TH BLOCK RUNNER

He replied, "Blessed rather are those who hear the word of God and obey it." (Luke 11:28 NIV)

You wait in utter silence. Your excitement pounds heavily in your chest and races through your body. Ready, get set go! You explode off the starting blocks with every fiber of your being and sprint down the track ahead.

In life, we may find ourselves lingering on the starting blocks waiting for God to use us. Guess what! God can use you! Right now, right where you are! It's time we stopped looking around and wondering what we can do and start taking immediate action! God put you where you are because that is where He wants to use you!

Today is the day we must ask God to open our eyes and hearts to how He wants to use us and then, it's time to get busy! You are passionate. You are dedicated. You are just the person God can use to do His will! So go, it's time to launch off the blocks and into the job God has called you to do!

APRIL 30TH CLUTTERED CLOSETS

Whoever pursues righteousness and love finds life, prosperity, and honor. (Proverbs 21:21 NIV)

It's time for spring cleaning! That's right; it's time to sort through the hodgepodge of stuff trapped in your house! A great way to start is by giving away those old running shoes you have haphazardly stacked in your hallway, closets, and garage. This is good news for you, when you decide to donate your gently used running shoes it helps someone who really needs them!

An excess of shoes in your house can easily be cleaned, but what do you do when your life is full of "stuff"? Brothers and sisters, it's time to "de-clutter" our lives with the extras and make more room for more Jesus! Clean up the stuff and the things and the obligations that leave you tired, empty, and overworked and fill those spaces with the love, joy, and peace of God!

MAY 1ST RUNNING THROUGH GOD'S GARDEN

See! The winter is past; the rains are over and gone. Flowers appear on the earth; the season of singing has come, the cooing of doves is heard in our land. (Song of Songs 2:11-12 NIV)

Inhale and exhale the aromatic fragrance of the gorgeous flowers all around you. Soak in the beauty of God's creation as flowers vibrantly display their pearly whites, splendid yellows, royal purples, and deep blues. Bumblebees, butterflies, and birds buzz excitedly all around you, bringing a sense of joy and excitement. The bright sun smiles on the earth below, gently melting the blanket of winter.

Running in spring is a true gift of God! The dead and dreariness of winter is transformed into the new beauty of spring. It offers breathtaking views for anyone outside. You can feel the love and warmth all around you as new life emerges and breaks free! Give thanks to God today for all the glorious works of His hands. Thank God for all His hands have created. Run in your King's grace and mercy today! Thank God for each and every beautiful step you are generously given!

MAY 2ND RUNNING ACTS OF KINDNESS

No one has ever seen God; but if we love one another, God lives in us and his love is made complete in us. (1 John 4:12 NIV)

When you think of helping others, "serving" as a runner probably doesn't immediately pop into your mind! But on second thought, as runners we are out and about "running into" so many people. We are going just slow enough to use opportunities to help others but just fast enough that if we do not seize the moment, it can pass us by.

Every day, our Maker graciously presents us with numerous moments to act in charitable kindness and tenderhearted love! Today while you are out on a run take advantage of being Christ's hands and feet. When you see someone who needs help, assistance, or maybe just a second of your time, take that time to generously show Christ's love. Eagerly take advantage of every chance God gives you to brighten and bring cheer to someone else. Make someone else's ordinary day an extraordinary day!

MAY 3RD PRAYER RUNNING

Pray continually, (1 Thessalonians 5:17 NIV)

Today is a day of prayer! Praying, which is probably the easiest thing we can do, is the one thing we do the least. So today we are going to change things! You have been given ample time during your run to do just that, pray! So during this time of pounding shoes and quick breaths, lift up your voice unto the Lord! Yahweh is so deserving of our praise!

That being said; don't let your prayers end with your run. Let your prayer filled running be a launching point for the rest of the day! Today is a day to take your time spent talking with God seriously. God loves you and wants to know what's on your heart. Talk to your Heavenly Father! God wants to hear what's on your heart!

MAY 4TH GUIDED RUNS

The way of fools seems right to them, but the wise listen to advice. (Proverbs 12:15 NIV)

Running with blinders on? Refusing to take advice from any voice other than your own? Failing to accept counsel can be detrimental, especially in running! It can be easy to fall into the trap of doing what we think is best and ending up injured and sitting out on sidelines. No fun!

Sound familiar? We so often as humans think we've got it all covered, totally under control. We think we are sailing smooth! Sometimes we are just too embarrassed to ask for help. We question what others will then think of us. However, it is not until we reach out and admit that we don't know it all, that others are able to swoop in and place a guiding and prudent hand on our shoulders. Everyone, at times, needs an insightful and sensible friend to come alongside us and point us in the direction of Christ. A wise friend and a helpful word are lovely gifts from God!

MAY 5TH RUN TO INSPIRE

"In the same way, let your light shine before others, that they may see your good deeds and glorify your Father in heaven." (Matthew 5:16 NIV)

You are an inspiration! Yes, You! As a runner, you influence others to lace up their sneakers and hit the open road. Close friends and family cannot even fathom what drives you to run all those miles every year day in and day out. As a highly motivated runner you can energize others to set goals with expectant hopes of achieving their dreams.

Along with your ability to motivate another to run, it is just as important to inspire another to live a life that glorifies God. Our Christian walk is not a life that should be run in secret, but lived like a light placed on a hill for all to see. You are like a city on a hill, shinning bright for all to see! So run, letting the light of Jesus shine inside of you, for all to see! Inspire on!

MAY 6ᵀᴴ I'M AN AUTHENTIC RUNNER

"This is to my Father's glory, that you bear much fruit, showing yourselves to be my disciples." (John 15:8 NIV)

Running shoes litter your hallway. Your worn running watch lies expectantly on your dresser. Water bottles lay stacked around your kitchen. Prized race medals decorate your bedroom. Sweaty workout clothes pile high inside your laundry room. Anyone who knows you can attest to your love for running. You are a legitimate, genuine runner! The evidence is stacked against you! From your house to your car to the rugged muscles silhouetted on your legs, your passion for running is a sure give away!

It's pretty obvious you are a runner but can others tell you are a Christian? Would others find enough evidence to prove you were a follower of Christ? Would your actions, words, and attitude prove your love for God? Would your life speak for itself?

MAY 7ᵀᴴ MORNING RUNS WITH OUR SAVIOR

In the morning, LORD, you hear my voice; in the morning I lay my requests before you and wait expectantly. (Psalm 5:3 NIV)

In the stillness of the morning, in the quietness of your run, this is a wonderful place to meet Jesus. It is in the tranquility of the morning we feel God near. Sometimes it's in these moments that we feel the closest to our Creator.

Between the stretch of the rising sun and the beauty of the light trickling through the darkness, you can gaze in wonder and awe in all God has created. We can be still and know that He is God. Our Maker has created these beautiful moments. Enjoy these peaceful moments knowing that craziness and busyness lie ahead of you today, appreciate the quietness of this time. As you begin to embark on your run today take the time to appreciate the gift of running and all God has placed in your life! Beginning your day with God is the best way to launch any day!

MAY 8ᵀᴴ JUST GETTING STARTED

I consider that our present sufferings are not worth comparing with the glory that will be revealed in us. (Romans 8:18 NIV)

Watch me do work! That's right; tell the world you are just getting started! This is only your warm up! You have great and glorious things you hope to do in Christ! Your feet have places to go and people to tell about the love, joy, and peace you have discovered in Jesus.

You might have run many sweaty, hard, and tortuous miles to get here, but that was nothing compared to what you have in Christ! Even when you feel tired, overwhelmed, and intimidated by the challenges around you, never grow faint of heart. Nope, you get your joy and energy from Christ, so no matter who or what comes against you, you are ready to run victoriously onward! So come alongside brothers and sisters, and let's do work for Christ!

MAY 9ᵀᴴ OVERNIGHT RUNNING SENSATION

I wait for the LORD, my whole being waits, and in his word I put my hope. I wait for the Lord more than watchmen wait for the morning, (Psalm 130:5-6a NIV)

Overnight champion? No way! Running takes diligent effort, ample time, and dedicated running, lots of running! Runners must gradually build their mileage base and carefully follow a training program. If instant results cannot occur in running, why do we expect immediate solutions in our daily lives?

Why do we so often expect our Heavenly Father to give us anything we want at the snap of our little fingers? We must be patient and wait on the Lord. His ways are perfect and God has the best plan for our lives. Just as you are persistent and determined to stick to a training schedule, diligently seek God and the plan He has for your life!

MAY 10ᵀᴴ JUST BECAUSE I RUN

Do not love the world or anything in the world. If anyone loves the world, love for the Father is not in them. (1 John 2:15 NIV)

Have you ever found yourself dreaming about food? You begin to reason. You ran five miles, so why can't you indulge your sweet tooth on a smorgasbord of ice cream? Or you ran this morning so you compliment yourself with free pass to veg out on the couch all day Saturday.

Ring a bell? How many of us have really meaningfully worshiped God at church and then walk out of the building to quickly fall into the ways of the world? We almost feel as if just because we are "good" and "go to church" we have a free pass to indulge in things we know are not good for us. Say no to a "just because attitude"! But we are called to live lives that emulate Jesus Christ, not the things of this world! We are to live our lives in complete submission to God. Because of God's love, goodness, and grace we will not want to have a "free pass" attitude but a "yes Lord" posture. We get to live our lives for Jesus! We get to love God and show His love to others! Have an attitude that reflects and imitates your gratitude!

MAY 11TH RUN TODAY!

Jesus answered, "I am the way and the truth and the life. No one comes to the Father except through me." (John 14:6 NIV)

Today is the day! The day you start your running adventure! You can do it! Do not fear, all you have to do is put one foot in front of the other! What was that? You think it's too late to begin? Nope! Never! It is never too late to become a healthier version of you!

Until your last breath, you have the chance, the gift, and the possibility to accept Jesus as your Lord and Savior! God loves you, just as you are. There is nothing that you have done in your past or present that can prevent the everlasting love and forgiveness of God from flooding every crack and corner of your heart.

It is not too late! Today is the day to say yes to a personal relationship with Jesus Christ! Say yes to Jesus! Today! What are you waiting for, run to Him, say yes to Jesus!

MAY 12TH RUNNING FOR YAHWEH'S GLORY

Not to us, LORD, not to us but to your name be the glory, because of your love and faithfulness. (Psalm 115:1 NIV)

Do you run with glorious visions of medals elegantly gracing your neck, your hands happily held high in the air in triumph, and your family and friends proudly congratulating you? Honestly, we probably have all marveled at this dream and wish acknowledgment for our all our hard work, sweat, and tears.

We desire to be the best parent. We seek to excel at our job. We hope to earn acknowledgment as the coolest friend, the friendliest neighbor, and the most compassionate family member. We try to be the Christian who is known for what you do within your church and the community. It is nice to get the credit where credit is due. However, it is important to ask ourselves one question. Are we doing these things for ourselves and for recognition, or for God's glory? Work, praise, volunteer, live and run to glorify God! It's all for God!

MAY 13ᵀᴴ MOM ON THE RUN

A wife of noble character who can find? She is worth more than rubies. Her husband has full confidence in her and lacks nothing of value. She brings him good, not harm, all the days of her life. (Proverbs 31:10-12 NIV)

Thank you moms for all you do! This is your special day and you so deserve it! Your tired feet are always on the run for all those precious souls God has placed in your tender care. Today is your day to pamper yourself and decide to take an extra long special run or take the day off and prop your feet up on a comfy sofa, your choice! You are a gift from God and He loves you so much!

You fill a special roll to the lives of everyone you touch. You have a beautiful heart and a desire to guide your household in a way that pleases your Heavenly Father. Thank you for all you do and all you continue to do! May you continue to seek God first in everything you do and may you continue to be a role model for those God has placed in your loving care!

MAY 14ᵀᴴ LACKING THE FAITH TO KEEP RUNNING

"So is my word that goes out from my mouth: It will not return to me empty, but will accomplish what I desire and achieve the purpose for which I sent it." (Isaiah 55:11 NIV)

Have the gas but lacking the go? Are you lacking the confidence to keep running? Feeling not fast enough, good enough, or strong enough? You feel as if you just cannot go on.

Life can mirror much the same. We feel useless as if even our best efforts fall flat. We become discouraged in our walk with Jesus. We fail to see the beautiful talents God has given us to serve Him, to share His love, and tell of His forgiveness with others. We forget that it is not our actions but the Holy Spirit working in us and through us. So when you become discouraged in your faith, in running, or in your life remember one important thing: you in your human nature may not be able to do it but you are not alone! You have the gift of the Holy Spirit living within you and with God, all things are possible! Never give up!

MAY 15ᵀᴴ IRONCLAD RUNNERS

As iron sharpens iron, so one person sharpens another. (Proverbs 27:17 NIV)

Come on ironclad runners! It's time to refine not only your own running skills but sharpen the skills of your fellow friend! Running together, nothing can stop you! We were not made to do life alone!

As Christians we have a community of fellow believers to love and support us, and for us to do the same! God made us to encourage, inspire, and help one other in our pursuit to Glorify God. Fellow brothers and sisters in Christ are waiting for someone, just like you, to laugh with, share with, and spur one another on in living lives that are pleasing to God. They just might be waiting for you to ask! Take the first step! In your running or in your faith walk, find someone to come alongside as a fellow comrade in Christ. Get to know them. Share your faith with them! What are you waiting for!

MAY 16TH RUNNING NAGS

What shall we say, then? Shall we go on sinning so that grace may increase? By no means! We are those who have died to sin; how can we live in it any longer? (Romans 6:1-2 NIV)

What area of running do you struggle through? Do you have a recurring injury that continually plagues your runs and sidelines your well meaning race plans? We all have trouble spots in our running, areas that delay our training plans.

Sin, like injuries, can affect your faith walk, when they continue to be repeated and un-repented. Continuing to choose to live in sin not only hurts us and others around us but also affects our relationship with God! Sins, like injuries are bad news, no matter how big or small! The God of the universe not only knows all but sees all! So confess your sin and turn from that trouble spot! No worldly pleasure compares to the true treasure found in Jesus Christ our Messiah.

MAY 17TH READY, SET...GO!

"Therefore go and make disciples of all nations, baptizing them in the name of the Father and of the Son and of the Holy Spirit, and teaching them to obey everything I have commanded you. And surely I am with you always, to the very end of the age." (Matthew 28:19-20 NIV)

As runners, we love the word "go". Running does not allow us just to sit there. We have to make the decision to get up and produce the effort for running. It is not necessarily an easy decision or even one that that has no cost attached, however in order to run, we have to go!

As Christians we also need to go, but go where? Different people are called to different places. For some, this literally might mean moving across the world, while others might be called to their coworker or their neighbor across the street. The "going" might look different for everyone but the fact that we must do something remains the same. We are called to step out in faith and share the hope that is only found in Jesus! As a runner this makes perfect sense. So today make an effort to "go" and "make" a disciple of Jesus Christ!

MAY 18TH RUNNING WITH INSECURITIES

I praise you because I am fearfully and wonderfully made; your works are wonderful, I know that full well. (Psalm 139:14 NIV)

We feel too thin, too fat, too slow, too un-athletic, too old, or maybe even too young. As runners we can feel any number of insecurities. You are boldly putting yourself out there and the persistent voice in our head begins to tell us all the things we cannot do! But whatever the uncertainty do not allow insecurities to barricade you from escaping your cozy couch!

In the same way we can let self doubt keep us from serving God. So often we see our highly talented Christian brothers and sisters and we quickly begin to look down on ourselves. We view what we perceive as our imperfections glaring at us in the mirror and in everything we do. We feel like we are not good enough, not smart enough, not strong enough, or that we do not know enough. During these feelings of inadequacy, it is important to see yourself for the extraordinary individual God created you to be! God created us all in His own image and He uniquely created each and every one of us for a special purpose. A special purpose that can be used to bring God glory! So run forward with the boldness and confidence that comes from God!

MAY 19TH RESTLESS HEART AND ACHY LEGS

My soul yearns for you in the night; in the morning my spirit longs for you. (Isaiah 26:9a NIV)

Darkness surrounds you. It is calmly silent except for the soothing tick of the hallway clock. You are the only one still awake in the quiet house with your exhausted mind begging for sleep. You would drift away into a dreamless sleep if it were not for your legs. As worn out as you may be, your achy legs are exasperatingly awake, restless as can be.

Many of life's irksome problems keep us awake at night. Financial setbacks, family arguments, and looming deadlines weave in and out of the tired mind keeping it awake and alert. So if counting white fluffy mammals has failed once again please consider another solution... turning your thoughts to God! Give God everything that has left you feeling weak and weary, restless and worn out. Worship

Him as you yearn for God within the confines of your bed. Love God, praise Him, and give thanks for all He is! So rest on that soft comfy pillow and sleep tight in your Creator's everlasting presence!

MAY 20TH I DON'T MISS RUNNING

"But be sure to fear the LORD and serve him faithfully with all your heart; consider what great things he has done for you." (1 Samuel 12:24 NIV)

You didn't run yesterday, the day before that, and not even the day before that. Maybe your last run wasn't just days ago but weeks or months ago! And the crazy thing is that you don't even miss it! Have you ever noticed the less you do something the less you start to miss it? When you are faithfully running every day you feel terrific. You start to look forward to your run, your clothes are fitting better, and you have an abundance of extra energy. Then somewhere along the way life gets hectic and running falls to the wayside.

Time spent with God can happen much the same way. At first you were excited, even ecstatic to spend time with God every day. You woke up thinking of God's mercies, met with Him during the day, and went to bed thanking Him for His blessings. But then life got in the way. You let your time with God become less and less, to almost nonexistent. Where did that spark go? How did the flame get snuffed out? Do not fear because today is a new day and you can get that fire back in your life! Make time to pray and thank your Heavenly Father for all of His blessings and you will feel that fire start to burn again!

MAY 21ST RUNNING THROUGH THE STORM

"When you pass through the waters, I will be with you; and when you pass through the rivers, they will not sweep over you. When you walk through the fire, you will not be burned; the flames will not set you ablaze." (Isaiah 43:2 NIV)

Boom! Bang! Crash! Lightning and thunder begins to erupt in the distance. The harsh wind begins to push and prod you along as if you were a rag doll. The warm rain wildly pelts your exposed face. You put up your hands to guard your face but to no avail, you need to find safe shelter and fast! Running in a storm is not only scary, it is downright dangerous! Quickly seeking protection and finding a place out of harm's way is your only solution.

Are you going through a storm or worse yet, a stormy season in your life? Because we live in a fractured and fallen world, scary and dangerous times in our lives are inevitable. However we have hope! Our hope, our shelter, and stronghold can only be found in Jesus. God might not necessarily stop the storm, but He will be there to get you through. Jesus is Lord over every storm, in your life.

MAY 22ND RUNNING LIKE CLOCKWORK

My soul yearns for you in the night; in the morning my spirit longs for you. (Isaiah 26:9a NIV)

You are a runner of habit! You do the same exact thing every day! You jump out of bed, down a light breakfast, hurriedly get dressed, and then it's go time! Running like clockwork is a great way to ensure you always get your workout in, but could there be something else even more important than a run that is not even making your daily to-do list?

Time with God should be the staple of your day, every day! Seeking God shouldn't just be done when we all of a sudden need Him. We need to long for God, knowing perfectly well that you could not take another step without Him! Our day should not feel right until we have spoken to our King, praised Him, and given Him our upmost admiration! We need God's peace, joy, and direction every second of every minute.

So as soon as you open your eyes, seek God. Make your time together a habit, like clockwork!

MAY 23RD JESUS THEN RUN

"However, I consider my life worth nothing to me; my only aim is to finish the race and complete the task the Lord Jesus has given me- the task of testifying to the good news of God's grace." (Acts 20:24 NIV)

You are a loving mom, dad, sister, or brother. You are an inspiring runner. You are a caring nurse. You are a fun teacher. You are a selfless stay-at- home parent. You are a courageous policeman. You are a bold fire fighter. You are a hard working lineman.

We all hold titles and tasks we must do, things we must complete. However the most important mission we are given in this life is to live a life that glorifies God. Living for God is something that we must do every day, with everything we are. Everything, literally everything must come second to God. Are you placing anything above Jesus? Your running, your family, your job, your own personal happiness or comfort? Place Jesus first in your life! Then, and only then, can everything else fall into place!

MAY 24TH RUNNING ALONGSIDE FLUFFY FRIENDS

Two are better than one, because they have a good return for their labor: (Ecclesiastes 4:9 NIV)

Woof Woof! Woof Woof! What's more enjoyable than running? Running with man's best friend, your dog! Running with Fido has so many benefits. Canines serve as serious motivation to run, offer camaraderie, and just give overall enjoyment. Many of you have had a really reliable, trusty tail-wagger that has touched your heart in some form or another.

A good dog is a splendid gift from our Heavenly Father, to which we should be deeply appreciative and highly thankful for! Have you thanked God lately for your fellow running partner? Thank God that He has put that big or little, slobbery or furry, sleepy or jumpy pooch in your life and enjoy every minute you have running with him or her.

MAY 25TH RUNNING BLISTERS

And wherever he went- into villages, towns or countryside- they placed the sick in the marketplaces. They begged him to let them touch even the edge of his cloak, and all who touched it were healed. (Mark 6:56 NIV)

Ouch! Ouch! Ouch! You rip off your socks and shoes to reveal what you already knew, an ugly blister! Blisters may be the body's way of protecting itself, but they most definitely hurt!

Sometimes as humans we build up high walls to protect ourselves from any further hurt, heart aches, and pains. At times we try to block everyone out and don't want to let anyone in. God already knows your pain and your hurts, but He wants you to bring it to Him. He wants your aches and pains. God has the soothing balm to alleviate your hurting heart. God is the Healer of all problems, give them to Him! Give God your ouches, your heartaches, and your worries today!

MAY 26TH RUN, SHARE, AND CARE

And do not forget to do good and to share with others, for with such sacrifices God is pleased. (Hebrews 13:16 NIV)

Runners run side by side. You are not running this race alone! By sharing your weakness as well your strengths, you become more approachable, and invite others in. Runners form a strong bond as they laugh and share their own mishaps, triumphs, and failures.

We can build and encourage each other as we run stride by stride!

As Christians we so often put on the persona that we are perfect. It is almost like we try to hide our struggles and our fears from others so they won't think less of us. We are afraid and sometimes even ashamed to reveal our many weaknesses. As brothers and sisters in Christ let us grow with each other in our maturity, increasingly seeking Jesus, and becoming closer to one another in His love! Let us put off our insecurities and encourage one another in everything we do! Let's run joyously together, hand in hand!

MAY 27TH MOUTH ON THE RUN

Yet to all who did receive him, to those who believed in his name, he gave the right to become children of God- (John 1:12 NIV)

"I just wasn't made to run." "I don't look like a runner." "I cannot do this." "I'm just not good enough!"Wait a second! What are you saying about yourself? It's time to get one very important thing straight! You, yes you, are loved, important, and made for a purpose. You are not the negative things you say or think about yourself. You have a Father in heaven who loves you just the way you are. God loves you so much that He sent His one and only Son so that you may have eternal life!

So it's time to change your tune! You can do anything you put your mind to! You can run! You can live for Christ! You can be the love of Christ for all to see! You can make a difference in this world! Believe in yourself, because God believes in you! You are loved!

MAY 28TH FREEDOM RUN

Thanks be to God for his indescribable gift! (2 Corinthians 9:15 NIV)

Not everyone can run, due to any number of physical and or mental limitations. If you are running right now, thank God for the ability to run!

Just like the freedom to run, you should find yourself blessed to live in a country where you have the freedom to worship Jesus. Not every person in every country has that awesome privilege. Today is a day to thank God for the veterans that have fought and have given their lives for our freedom. Thank God for the service men and women that have sacrificed their lives for our independence!

Pray for blessings on their family and friends and that they would know Jesus as their Lord and Savior. Also pray for Jesus followers around the world who are being persecuted and imprisoned for their faith right now! Pray that God would use faithful and bold servants to proclaim His love where darkness and hopelessness exist. Utilize that well fought for freedom to boldly and confidently pray, give, and encourage our brothers and sisters around the globe!

MAY 29TH A WORD OF RUNNING MOTIVATION

"The grass withers and the flowers fall, but the word of our God endures forever." (Isaiah 40:8 NIV)

Words inspire us. They push us. They revitalize us. They kindle and fuel a roaring fire within us. God's Word is a motivator for us. Nurturing us, cheering us on, loving and building us up to be more Christ like every day. To invigorate you on your run today write out Bible verses on cards that inspire you, verses that fill your heart with hope and confidence.

Then strategically place those encouraging cards on your mirror, on top of your running shoes, or attach them on your door to read before you head out. Try writing down several verses and post them on and around your treadmill. In the same way you can bring encouragement to a friend. Uplift others by writing down scripture and posting them where they will be seen throughout the day. Run with the encouragement and love of God's Word in your heart today! Share the beautiful words you wish to hear.

MAY 30TH MIND ON THE RUN

You will keep in perfect peace those whose minds are steadfast, because they trust in you. (Isaiah 26:3 NIV)

A tall glass of water, filled to the brim with ice, enticingly sweats on the kitchen counter. Hmmm, better yet make that a pepperoni pizza, with lots of cheese. Yes, lots of cheese or even better, make it a burger. A gigantic burger brimming with French fries! Thoughts of dinner distracting you while running? Perhaps instead of food, your mind fixates on a beautiful sparkling pool with a relaxing raft reserved just for you!

Running isn't the only place we find ourselves distracted by our thoughts. How often have you found yourself dreaming about lunch while sitting in church listening to the sermon? How often do we let our hearts wander while praising God? It's time to focus our hearts, minds, eyes, ears, and toes on the God of the universe. It's time to give God your total and undivided attention today!

MAY 31ST RUNNING FROM THE HEART

My flesh and my heart may fail, but God is the strength of my heart and my portion forever. (Psalm 73:26 NIV)

You have to dig down deep. Way down deep to keep up this vigorous pace. You have to run from deep within! Not only with your muscles and not only with your strength but with your heart! Deep from within, from your devoted love for running! When you run, you run from the heart! If you didn't, you would not make it very far!

Living for God is much the same way.

We should seek to glorify, serve, and zealously seek God with all of our hearts! Love and live for God in a way that is desperate, as if you could not breathe if He was not in your air. We must fervently walk in a way that is earnest, seeking rest within God's presence. We must fanatically love God with our whole hearts, with everything and every fiber of our being. God is our King, He is our Creator, and He is worthy of all our love and praise! Intensely live for God with all your heart!

JUNE 1ST IT'S MORE THAN JUST RUNNING

"Then you will call upon me and come and pray to me, and I will listen to you. You will seek me and find me when you seek me will all your heart." (Jeremiah 29:12-13 NIV)

Wait! You want more than just my Sunday? Living for Christ demands so much more than just parking in a seat every Sunday. So much more! It's a 24/7, minute by minute, all in walk with our Savior all year long. When we say yes to Jesus, we say yes to submitting our lives to Him. We are all in!

As a runner, you can understand this! Running entails so much more than just the physical act of trotting down the sidewalk. Runners stretch, strengthen, cross-train, eat healthy, research and buy the best running gear. Not to mention all the time spent talking about running! So keep your shoes on and ready to do the will of your Heavenly Father! Be Christ's hands and feet each and every second and everywhere you go!

JUNE 2ND LONELY RUNNING

"The LORD himself goes before you and will be with you; he will never leave you nor forsake you. Do not be afraid; do not be discouraged." (Deuteronomy 31:8 NIV)

The soft thud of shoes methodically hits the pavement. You run alone down the middle of a tree lined path to the even patter of your favorite shoes. Are you running alone? Perhaps you have searched high and low for someone else to run with and cannot find even one. Maybe you have found a fellow runner but your paces or daily schedules are so vastly different you are unable to keep up with each other.

Life can get lonely sometimes. There are so many reasons we feel alone in life but it is vital to remember that you are never alone. God is always there! God is there when you wake up, when you go to work, when you drive your car, when you run, and even while you make dinner. Always watching over you and always protecting you! You are never running alone!

JUNE 3ʳᵈ YOU ARE A WINNER!

But thanks be to God! He gives us the victory through our Lord Jesus Christ. (1 Corinthians 15:57 NIV)

Drum roll please! Announcing all winners, please stand up. Well…stand up! You! Yes you! You have already won in Christ! When you accept Jesus as your Lord and Savior you have won the free gift of salvation that is only offered through faith in Christ Jesus. This wondrous gift of salvation is nothing we have worked for, sweated for, or even deserve. The beautiful gift of salvation requires absolutely nothing on our part except faith. Just believe in Jesus as your Lord! That's it, that's all! Sounds pretty simple doesn't it? That's because it is!

So run today like the winner you already are! Run with the blessed assurance of knowing God loves you and cares for you. You can run with the pure joy of knowing that no matter what happens you have already won! You are treasured child of God and He has great plans for you!

JUNE 4ᵀᴴ DON'T WALK, RUN!

"But you will receive power when the Holy Spirit comes on you; and you will be my witnesses in Jerusalem, and in all Judea and Samaria, and to the ends of the earth." (Acts 1:8 NIV)

You glance to your left. You gaze to your right. The person on your left is enthusiastically head bobbing to music as they loudly pound away on the tread-mill. The person to your right is doing much the same. Except this runner, is not only listening to music but watching the news, texting, and periodically thumbing through a magazine as she mildly jogs along. Sharing the gospel with someone else can seem impossible at times. You might literally be right next to them and still not have the opportunity to share. So how do you tell about Christ's love while hurdling over headphones, cell phones, TV screens, and unwelcoming stares?

Perhaps the person next to you isn't running on a treadmill but is sitting inside a cubicle or taking your order in a restaurant. It can scary to engage the person next to you but God has planted them right next to you for a reason! Remember it is not your words but God's words! So start by listening to that person, share your story, and then tell of God's glory. Don't walk, but run to share the good news!

JUNE 5ᵀᴴ WORKING UP A SWEAT

In the same way, faith by itself, if it is not accompanied by action, is dead. (James 2:17 NIV)

Wipe that brow! You are working hard and it shows! Sweat runs from the top of your head to your toes! Running demands sweat and lots of it! Running necessitates action and requires the runner to give his or her all! Living for Jesus also entails sweat. Faith requires us to roll up our sleeves and love others with the same love Jesus shows us!

"We love because he first loved us." (1 John 4:19 NIV)

It may seem impossible to love others. It may seem the more you love them the more unloving they act. Yes it can be very hard and demanding and require a lot of work. Just remember Christ loves you for who you are and who you were. There may have been times when you were hard to love. Do your best to give others the same grace Christ gives you. Having a servant's heart may require hard work but it will definitely be worth it!

JUNE 6ᵀᴴ RUNNERS EVERYWHERE

As a prisoner for the Lord, then, I urge you to live a life worthy of the calling you have received. (Ephesians 4:1 NIV)

Which of the following best describes you as a runner; a crazy daily, strong weekend warrior, or a new year's dreamer? Every runner holds a varying level of commitment and dedication.

Like runners, there seem to be a wide variety to the commitments of Christians. The great news is that all Christians who have accepted Jesus as their Lord and Savior are saved by the blood of Jesus. But as we grow as children of God, we desire to seek Him more and more, to grow more and more like Jesus. As we mature, we become abundantly aware of our need for Jesus and the unlimited mercy and grace of God's love. Because of this, we cannot help but eagerly seek more and more of Him. It is impossible to contain the joy we find in Christ! We desire to do everything and anything we can to glorify God! So run eagerly, passionately seeking to share the joy of what Christ has done in our lives!

JUNE 7TH RUNNING WITH HALLELUIAHS!

Rejoice in the Lord always. I will say it again: Rejoice! (Philippians 4:4 NIV)

Running with a smile is probably easier said than done! Most runners usually break into their happy dance only after completing their grueling workout! As a challenge for today: make a point to run as a fountain of gladness and joy! When your insides are full of thankfulness, the love you have inside is sure to transpire to the outside, for the whole world to see!

God loves you so much! God has a special plan for you and your life! Be jubilant knowing that everything is in God's trustworthy hands! Celebrate that you can run! Rejoice knowing you have breath in your lungs and life in your body. Spread that joy and happiness with whomever you can! Rejoice in God's love, in whatever your hands and feet find to do!

JUNE 8TH MY RUNNING PRAYER

"You may ask me for anything in my name, and I will do it." (John 14:14 NIV)

Heavenly Father, thank You. Thank You for your goodness and love that you shower down from above. Teach us your ways Lord, that I may run in your paths, and take the roads of life that are pleasing to you. Thank You for the gift of running. Thank You for the blessing of enjoyment and joy that only comes from You. Show me how to run in a way that brings glory and honor to You. Heavenly Father, thank You for Your faithfulness. Thank you for staying beside me every step I take. Thank You for Your continued protection, Your mercy, and Your grace.

Open my eyes Lord to those around me today. Help me to see others as You see them. Shape my heart in a way that is loving, generous, and thankful to those you have placed in my path today. Please grant me the opportunity to share Your love. I ask that You would use my legs today to live in a way that glorifies You. Please guide my steps in a direction that pleases You and points others to Your Son. In Jesus Name, Amen.

JUNE 9TH RUNNING BLUNDERS

Blessed is the one whose sin the LORD does not count against him and in whose spirit is no deceit. (Psalm 32:2 NIV)

Your stomach feels like a roaring sea monster. You kick yourself for eating that extra cheese pizza right before running! This mistake only adds to a lengthy checklist of running blunders such as, forgetting to stretch (ohh!), wearing the wrong shoes (ouch!), failing to use the bathroom (uh oh!), forgetting your water bottle (boo!), and running too hard, too fast (yikes!).

Life is full of slip ups! The great thing about our failures and mishaps is that we have a Heavenly Father who will not hold them against us! When we truly ask God for forgiveness, He forgives us. God washes our sins away. They are gone!

"Though your sins are like scarlet, they shall be as white as snow; though there are red as crimson, they shall be like wool." (Isaiah 1:18b NIV)

We can confidently move forward without feeling condemned. We can boldly run without ever hesitantly glancing behind!

JUNE 10TH RUNNING NEW EVERY MORNING

Yet this I call to mind and therefore I have hope: Because of the LORD's great love we are not consumed, for his compassions never fail. They are new every morning; great is your faithfulness. (Lamentations 3:21-23 NIV)

You feebly crawl into bed and tuck your covers up around your head. You literally ache from nose to toes. As you lay wide awake in bed you start to wonder. How are you ever going to get up the next day, much less, run again? But as the morning light begins to trickle in under your shades, something amazing happens! You pop up in bed, feeling completely renewed and utterly refreshed! A little tired, sure; a little achy, perhaps; but you pull the covers aside and head out to begin a new day.

You know why? Because God's compassions never fail, they are new every morning. Every morning! That means every night we might go to bed feeling exhausted and worn out but we can leap out of our beds every day knowing our Father loves us and that our hope is in Him! Because of God's faithfulness and His love we have the promise of a new day! Good morning God!

JUNE 11ᵀᴴ FINISH STRONG!

I can do all this through him who gives me strength. (Philippians 4:13 NIV)

The deafening boom of the starting gun shatters the silence of a dark and silent morning. A herd of runners charge down the pathway like wild animals. You aggressively pump your legs like an exploding firecracker as a rush of excited energy flows through your body. Then the thoughts begin to start, flooding your mind with positive optimism, at this pace you will not only make record time but find your way in the winner's circle! But then miles later you start to fall apart and quickly! Your speedy sprint quickly falls to a swift run to a fading trot and then to a slow jog.

In life, we often start strong and quickly begin to putter out. But do not lose hope! The same Spirit that raised Jesus from the dead is living inside of you! So in all things, do not be afraid and do not lose hope, because with God, all things are possible! No matter what the obstacle, no matter what the pace, and no matter what roadblock stands in your way, through Christ we can find joy and peace through all circumstances!

JUNE 12ᵀᴴ RUNNING PLATEAUS

"You are the salt of the earth. But if the salt loses its saltiness, how can it be made salty again? It is no longer good for anything, except to be thrown out and trampled underfoot." (Matthew 5:13 NIV)

Have you hit a plateau? Has your running become stale, lifeless? Perhaps you feel as if running is no longer fun but has turned into a chore you just have to do every single day. Stuck in a rut and losing that exciting zest you once had, can easily make running a nightmare! Don't worry, you are not alone. Many runners have had that feeling at one time or another.

Ever feel the same way in your faith walk? Feel as if you have stopped growing and maturing in your faith? As though you have lost your zeal, your saltiness for Jesus? Hold up! It's time to ask ourselves, not where is God, but where am I? Where am I placing my passion? Am I placing anything above or before Jesus?

Following Jesus is simple. God first, everything else second, this is our Father's command to us! Keep praying, keep reading God's Word, and keep helping and showing others the love of Christ!

JUNE 13TH STICK TO YOUR RUNNING PLAN

Being confident of this, that he who began a good work in you will carry it on to completion until the day of Christ Jesus. (Philippians 1:6 NIV)

What happened? You were doing so great! Then all of a sudden you took a left turn, right off of your training plan! You started out strong. You were excited, diligently keeping to that pre-determined schedule. You were logging some serious miles and you were feeling great! But then somewhere along the way life happened!

How often in life do we start something with the best intentions and then miserably fail to finish? On top of this list is time spent with God. We so often tell ourselves that we are going to commit time in prayer, in God's Word, and in worship. Then once life gets busy and bumpy our faithful commitment to God is the first thing that falls to the wayside. So today be encouraged to confidently stay the course! Unlike running, you can never spend too much time with God!

JUNE 14TH RUN LIKE A MUSTARD SEED

He replied, "Because you have so little faith. Truly I tell you, if you have faith as small as a mustard seed, you can say to this mountain, 'Move from here to there' and it will move. Nothing will be impossible for you." (Matthew 17:20-21 NIV)

A mustard seed! Have you ever seen a mustard seed? It is a little bigger than a period on this page. If you held one in your hand you might drop it and not even know. Can you believe that faith as small as a mustard seed can move a mountain! A mountain! Do you have faith? Most importantly faith in Jesus Christ as our Lord and Savior but also faith in who God has created you to be. A faith that has confidence in the skills and talents God has graciously placed inside you. Believe in yourself! The Holy Spirit lives inside of you! That's right! Inside of you!

Live out your faith in confidence! Dream big! You, through the help of the Holy Spirit, can do anything, go anywhere! So run, do not walk! Use this hope to live in a way that glorifies God! Run that race in a way that centers around Jesus. Train for God. Run for God! And when you conqueror your mountain, give all the glory and honor to the Maker of Heaven and Earth!

JUNE 15TH A GLOAT-A-THON

Do not gloat when your enemy falls; when they stumble, do not let your heart rejoice, (Proverbs 24:17 NIV)

We all have a friendly rival, that fellow competitor that keeps us on our toes and drives us to run our very best! They make us run better, train harder, and give our all. But moment of truth, how do you feel when you beat that cordial challenger? Do you secretly win twice, once for completing and second for gloating over your adversary?

But we are not called to cheer when our enemy falls but to pick them up and encourage them, and be a loving cheerleader for whomever God places in your life. It's not always easy to love others but that should never stop us from trying! When you are feeling low on patience, cheer, forgiveness, or kindness all we have to do is pray! Ask the God of the universe to fill you up with His love, mercy, and grace! Ask God to allow you be the reflection of His love shining through you!

JUNE 16TH RUNNING TO CHANGE

"And if your right hand causes you to stumble, cut it off and throw it away. It is better for you to lose one part of your body than for your whole body to go into hell." (Matthew 5:30 NIV)

Let's admit it. You have passionately and fervently done everything in your control to heal.

You've been to the doctor, "Ah!" You've iced, "Brr!" You've rested, "Zzz!" You've elevated, "Oh!" You've even stopped running, "Boo!"

You have wholeheartedly followed everything your doctor said to the letter in hopeful efforts of being cleared to run again! But how often do we take an injury that prevents us from running much more seriously than something that affects our walk with the Lord?

Do you quickly repent and turn from your sin or do you just continue to allow these struggles keep you on the sidelines of your spiritual race? Let us live in a way that throws off all that hinders and ties us down, everything that keeps us from living a joyous life in Christ, while we faithfully and passionately run the race He has set before us!

JUNE 17TH RUNNING WITH DAD

As a father has compassion on his children, so the LORD has compassion on those who fear him; (Psalm 103:13 NIV)

He happily took your hand as you both wildly ran hand in hand around the backyard, and then erupted into laughs as you both fell into a pile of leaves. He proudly smiled at you as he ran beside you as you wholeheartedly pedaled your brand new bike down the driveway. He faithfully ran beside you as you eagerly trained for your very first school race and then again as you diligently trained for your first half marathon.

Thank you Dads for all you do and all the amazing love you show! We pray and ask continued guidance and direction in your lives and how you can continue to show the love of the Father to those God has placed in your life. Remember to always run close to your Heavenly Father and always put Him first in all you do!

JUNE 18TH ENCOURAGING RUNNER

"Give, and it will be given to you. A good measure, pressed down, shaken together and running over, will be poured in your lap. For with the measure you use, it will be measured to you." (Luke 6:38 NIV)

Are you a giving runner? A what! A runner who does not solely run for themselves but for others! Running in a way that overflows with Christ love for others! So what's the first step? Discover opportunities God has placed all around you to give of yourself and your talents. Looking for ideas? Find a friend. Almost everyone knows someone else who wants to run.

So run with them! Be their unending source of motivation and confidence. Lovingly run alongside them every step of the way. What if running is too much at first for them? No problem. Remember this isn't about your workout, but theirs! So start right where they are at a walk! A kind word and an encouraging smile can go a long way! Get those feet busy for Christ!

JUNE 19TH RUNNING WILD

"I am with you and will watch over you wherever you go, and I will bring you back to this land. I will not leave you until I have done what I have promised you." (Genesis 28:15 NIV)

Wow! Look at the mileage you put in this week! Tracking your running is a great way to motivate and encourage your training progress!

But where would your running watch track you when you were not running? Would it map out a life that glorifies God and proves a life lived for Christ? Or would it chart out places, things, and activities that hinder your walk with Christ? But be encouraged in this, that whatever you do and wherever you go, God is there! God loves you and desires to have a relationship with you today! God has great plans for you and your life! Let your steps sing of God's great love for you!

Let the places you go and the people you see know of God's amazing grace! God is faithfully and lovingly watching over each and every step you take!

JUNE 20ᵀᴴ GOOD BYE RUNNING

"Even to your old age and gray hairs I am he, I am he who will sustain you. I have made you and I will carry you; I will sustain you and I will rescue you." (Isaiah 46:4 NIV)

Whew! You are calling it quits! You tiredly wipe your brow as you eagerly make the decision to never run again! Have you ever tried to convince yourself that you were never running again? Perhaps it was after a devastating loss, an impossible race, or a life changing injury. Maybe something has happened in your life and you just don't feel like you can take another step. Perhaps you are going through a loss, divorce, money trouble, job change, or a fight and struggle with a loved one.

We have all felt this way a time or two. We get knocked down and feel zapped of the strength needed to get back up again. Whatever you might be going through, God is there. God loves you, and He will sustain you. It might seem like you will never get through this trial. Just remember, God is there through it all. Cast your burdens on God; ask for the strength and wisdom to make it through your time of struggle. God will give it to you! He will carry you through!

JUNE 21ˢᵀ JUST RUN WITH IT!

Now to him who is able to do immeasurably more than all we ask or imagine, according to his power that is at work within us, (Ephesians 3:20 NIV)

Can you run? If yes, that's awesome! If not, how will you ever know, until you try? You never know if you can run until you, well, run! Not until you tie your shoes and head out on the sidewalk or down the road, you have no idea of what you are capable of! So often we hold ourselves back and assure ourselves that there is no way, no how, that you would ever be able to run that long, that far. We frustrate our own plans! But once we gather our confidence and command our shoes to the ground we quickly discover something. We realize, we can run!

Faith is much the same. As humans we tend to hide in the shadows unsure and uncertain of all we can do. But it's time to live our faith out loud! To loudly proclaim all that Christ has done for you in your life! God has given us skills and talents that are unique to each and every one of us! Today is the day to optimize those talents and put them to good use, a use that glorifies and worships our Father in heaven!

JUNE 22ND PROUD TO BE A RUNNER

"Make a tree good and its fruit will be good, or make a tree bad and its fruit will be bad, for a tree is recognized by its fruit." (Matthew 12:33 NIV)

"Hey! You run, right?" You probably get this all the time! Everyone seems to recognize you as you run around your hometown. You are an instant hit when you walk into any store, gym, or restaurant. Friendly neighbors wave and smile at you as you pass by in your usual pair of running shoes and shorts as you energetically bob down the sidewalks.

They might know you as the runner, but do they know that you as a Christian? Hmmm…that can be kind of tricky. It's easy to tell you are a runner but can others see Christ living in you? Do your words and actions point others to Christ? Can you not help but declare all the wonderful things Jesus has done? Living the life of a Christian is not meant to be kept secret. Live it out loud! Excitedly run down the streets for Jesus, declaring His name and all He has done!

JUNE 23RD RUNNING FOR COVER

He will cover you with his feathers, and under his wings you will find refuge; his faithfulness will be your shield and rampart. (Psalm 91:4 NIV)

You watch them roll in. The looming dark clouds start to sail in like a fleet of ships on the sea. The wind starts to show its strength as it wildly tugs and pushes you along the sidewalk. The trees start to show their dismay with their creaks and groans. You need to find shelter and fast. Like many summer storms, this squall came out of no-where! The light rain turns into cold drops that fall heavily at your feet. You sprint to your door, just as the first crash of lightening illuminates the sky. Whoa, just in the nick of time!

Where do you run when the storms of life pop up out of the blue? Do you find yourself running alone in life's storm, drenched by the rain, and tossed by the wind? Or do you seek shelter in God's faithful arms, under His veil of protection? Run under the cover of God's loving embrace through all life's storms!

JUNE 24TH TENTATIVELY RUNNING

"The LORD does not look at the things people look at. People look at the outward appearance, but the LORD looks at the heart." (1 Samuel 16:7b NIV)

Your legs, your feet, your smile, your hair, your tummy, your nose, your arms, or your eyes can all be the problem. Anything from your body, or your clothes, or how you run can make you feel self conscious. Sometimes we let the opinions of others stop us from running.

Worse yet, we let it affect how we live for Christ. We feel the gazes of others. We smell their judgment. We shrink back in fear, afraid to step out in our faith. But hold up! We live to please God not man! It doesn't matter how others view you or even how you see yourself. It's about how God sees you! And God sees you as a perfect creation. So perfect you are one of a kind. There is no one else like you on the whole Earth! That's how special you are! As a child of God you can run in a way that reflects God's beauty that lives inside of you!

JUNE 25TH RUNNING WITH THE WRONG PACK

Do not be misled: "Bad company corrupts good character." (1 Corinthians 15:33 NIV)

Mmm Mmm Mmm! Just because you cherish indulging in that tasty sugary snack doesn't necessarily mean it's good for you! Living on a diet of empty calories probably isn't the wisest way to appropriately fuel you on your runs! Proper nutrition and what you put into your mouth can either hinder or push you on the next level.

Just like your diet can affect your health, what you do and those you surround yourself with could be affecting your walk with Jesus. It's time to ask yourself if the movies and television shows you are watching and the music you are hearing are influencing your walk with God. Are you "running" where you should not run or "running" with someone you know is hindering and even pulling you away from a closer relationship with God?

JUNE 26TH RUNNING SCHEDULES

Commit your way to the LORD; trust in him and he will do this: He will make your righteous reward shine like the dawn, your vindication like the noonday sun. (Psalm 37:5-6 NIV)

Your running plan is right where you can see it. It is posted perfectly center on your refrigerator door to remind you of tomorrow's workout. Covering your calendar lies the red Xs to mark off your accomplishments. The upcoming miles are written in bold black just waiting to be conquered .

But in your everyday life, whose plan do you have posted high and centered; yours or God's? What would your life look like if you were following God's will and seeking His agenda for your life? Would your day's outline look much the same or would that mean some bigger, bolder, and gustier moves on your part? It's time we gave our plans to God and asked Him to fill in our days! Let God determine your steps and your future!

JUNE 27TH ONE MOUTHY RUN

Do not let any unwholesome talk come out of your mouths, but only what is helpful for building others up according to their needs, that it may benefit those who listen. (Ephesians 4:29 NIV)

It's the unspeakable, unavoidable, and the cumbersome truth for us runners; it's perfectly possible to have "to go" when you are on "the go". Running in and out of port potties not only is annoying but costly to the numbers on the race clock!

But what is worse than running to and from the bathroom? A mouth on the run! Gossiping and talking about others not only hurts them, but hurts you! Guard not only your heart but your tongue! Let only words that bring praise to God, encouragement to others, and the story of Christ's love flow from your lips!

JUNE 28TH PERSONAL BESTS

Therefore, I urge you, brothers and sisters, in view of God's mercy, to offer your bodies as a living sacrifice, holy and pleasing to God-this is your true and proper worship. (Romans 12:1 NIV)

Congratulations! You have reached your ultimate goal! In running we strive to beat our own personal record. As runners, we continually strive to improve our running and demolish our old times. We give running our best. We give it our all. We will literally try almost anything to get our times down from training harder, running longer, to even changing our diets.

Do you give God your personal best? Do you give Him your all or just your tired and achy leftovers? We are called to glorify God with all of our hearts, with all of our minds, and with all that we are. We are to be living sacrifices to the perfect God we serve. Run for God in such a way that brings God all the glory and honor. Run for your King with all your heart, with all your soul, and with all your strength!

JUNE 29TH RUNNING: A FAITHFUL FRIEND

"I no longer call you servants, because a servant does not know his master's business. Instead, I have called you friends, for everything that I learned from my Father I have made known to you." (John 15:15 NIV)

Is running your old friend? Your faithful buddy that is always there eagerly waiting for you to slip into your shoes and travel to a place where you can just be yourself?

As we continue to walk with Jesus, He becomes more and more like an old, familiar friend. A faithful friend, who knows and understands your thoughts, your struggles, and your frustrations. An understanding companion who laughs with you through the good and who lovingly throws His arms around you when you need a good cry.

In running, it's not always about the distance but the run; and with Jesus, it's much the same. Jesus wants a relationship with you! A loving relationship where you look forward to spending time alone with Him! God is like the faithful friend who is always only one phone call away and who is always willing to hear everything that is weighing on your heart and mind. Jesus is always there. Always faithful! Jesus is waiting to be your friend!

JUNE 30TH CELEBRATE THE SMALL STEPS

The LORD has done it this very day; let us rejoice and be glad. (Psalm 118:24 NIV)

Throw the festive confetti! Don your party hat! Yes toot your own horn! This calls for a celebration. It's time to celebrate how far you have come, instead of the distance you still have to go! As a runner we have to learn to appreciate each and every accomplishment, no matter how big or how small it is! Commemorate finishing that first run, running twenty minutes straight, or losing your first five lbs! This calls for celebrating each and every milestone no matter what size!

It is the little things that count, the little things that we can be thankful for! As a follower of Jesus Christ we are surrounded by them! Each and every day God continues to abundantly bless us with brightly colored presents, like our family, friends, forgiveness, and grace! We just have to take the time to see them! To appreciate them! And thank our Father in heaven who so abundantly blesses us! Every day is a reason to celebrate God's everlasting love!

JULY 1ST PASSIONATELY RUNNING

"Do not worship any other god, for the LORD, whose name is Jealous, is a jealous God." (Exodus 34:14 NIV)

Wow! You are a firecracker! The enthusiasm and tenacity you have for running really shines through! Look at you go! Following Jesus also requires enthusiasm, a passionate fire for God! When you ask Jesus to be the Lord and Savior of our lives He wants all of us! All of our hearts! All of our desires!

For our "God is a consuming fire." Hebrews 12:29 (NIV)

Our God is a jealous God! So although it is awesome to be zealous about running, it is even more important to keep that zest in perspective. To never let our fervor for running, or anything else, exceed our passion for God! Seek God every day with every piece and fiber of your being! True joy is found in Jesus and in Him alone. Let your passion for Christ brightly shine for all to see!

JULY 2ND RUN STREET SMART

Be alert and of sober mind. Your enemy the devil prowls around like a roaring lion looking for someone to devour. (1 Peter 5:8 NIV)

"Wait! What's that noise?" You ask as you nervously glance over your shoulder and pick up the pace.

You heavily sigh in relief when you realize it was only a cute little squirrel scampering among the green bushes. You swallow hard and cautiously carry on. The area you are running through is unknown, the sun is setting, and your imagination is starting to run wild!

Running alone, in the dark, or through un-friendly areas can be not only be unsafe but downright dangerous. And as vital as it is to run street smart, it is more important to stay alert to the devil's attacks. He is a roaring lion seeking whom he may devour! It's time to stand firm in our faith, staying alert to the areas in your life that draw you into sin and away from God! This can be tough. It is a rough world out there, full of things and people that pull us off track and away from God, but hold tight to God, because He is holding tight to you! Stand firm and fasten tightly to God's everlasting love!

JULY 3RD RUNNING AGAINST ROADBLOCKS

We are hard pressed on every side, but not crushed; perplexed, but not in despair; persecuted, but not abandoned; struck down, but not destroyed. (2 Corinthians 4:8-9 NIV)

You are unstoppable! You are being pushed against from all sides and yet you boldly run on! You charge forward when others tell you otherwise. You dig your heels in and run on no matter what and no matter who comes against you! What staggering odds are stacked against you right now? What are you running against?

Are you struggling just to keep your head above water in your marriage, in your health, in your finances? When everything seems to be falling apart there is only one place where we can turn. To God! In Christ we will find the strength to not only get over the hurdle but discover the true peace and joy that comes hand in hand when you trust in God. So whatever you find yourself running against remember one thing, God is there. God's hands are outstretched waiting to clasp your timid fingers! Run with Jesus!

JULY 4TH FIRECRACKER RUNNER!

"So if the Son sets you free, you will be free indeed." (John 8:36 NIV)

It's time to celebrate and remember America's Independence! This independence came at the high cost of many lives and bloodshed so that we could have our freedom. Our salvation also came at a high price, the ultimate price! Jesus, the perfect and sinless Son of God, took all of our sins and nailed them to the cross. Christ's death and resurrection promise a life and freedom that can only come through faith in Him! We are free!

Run today not only appreciative and thankful for our nation's freedom but also for the freedom we have through Christ Jesus! So run patriotically in that freedom today and don't forget to celebrate this festive holiday around tasty food, with great friends, while encouraging each other on with the faith that is only found in Christ Jesus. Be a firecracker for Christ, for all to see!

JULY 5TH RUNNING LIKE A QUEEN BEE

Through Jesus, therefore, let us continually offer to God a sacrifice of praise-the fruit of lips that openly profess his name. (Hebrew 13:15 NIV)

You curl your upper lip and begin to pout. Big time! You pray every day, faithfully read your Bible, diligently attend church, and yet somehow you find yourself unable to do what you love. Run! You deserve better. Right?

But this is not really true though is it? Our God is a Father who blesses us generously and gives us far more than we ever deserve and heaps blessing upon blessing upon us each and every day! What did we do to deserve these blessings? Nothing! It is because of God's love and His love alone! Not because of anything we did but because of everything God does! So the next time you are angry that God did not allow you to get a faster time on that run or prevent you from being injured, stop and thank Him for all that He has done! Turn your sadness into thankfulness! Your frustration into praise! And sing your praises to The One who did it all on the cross!

JULY 6ᵀᴴ RUN BEFORE NOT AFTER

"Maratha, Martha," the Lord answered, "you are worried and upset about many things, but few things are needed-or indeed only one." (Luke 10:41-42a NIV)

The clock chimes, persistently reminding you that you are running out of time. You look around. Dirty dishes haphazardly line not only the sink, but around the kitchen table. Clothes lay in neat piles around the house, waiting to be put away. The living room floor lies littered with a montage of debris, needing to be placed in its perspective order. You sigh in eager desperation. Your house is literally a pig sty! You futilely stare out the window and realize that like the fading of the afternoon sun, the likelihood of fitting in your run today is also fading. Putting off your daily run can easily become a routine, can't it? We begin our mornings in hopeful expectations and then somewhere, along with our day, our best intentions become quickly derailed. However, you may be putting off more than just your run.

Are you also putting off time with God? You reason that there's just too much to do and that you cannot possibly come and meet your Heavenly Father until everything is neat and tidy. But in reality, life is never done! So come as you are, open and ready for God's love, and you will always leave better than you came! Refuel on God's love for you and then tackle the rest of your day!

JULY 7ᵀᴴ RUNNING BACK FOR MORE

I pray that out of his glorious riches he may strengthen you with power through his Spirit in your inner being, (Ephesians 3:16 NIV)

Calling yesterday a grueling workout, would be labeling it lightly! You emerged home from yesterday's run rosy cheeked, breathing hard, and ready for a time out! But even so, today is a new day and you find yourself willing, ready, and eager for more! You are achy, tired, and just hanging in there, but you put your shoes to the road and follow through on your workout!

Hey! Good for you! Coming back for another helping of hard work is never easy and not for the faint of heart!

When life lets us down, it can be difficult to come back for more. We get passed over at work, we get treated unkindly by others, and even our best efforts go unrecognized. Even so, we will never let anybody or anything, hold us down! We have the strength of God living inside us and through Him we have the strength and power to succeed! With God on our side, who can hold you down?

JULY 8TH EMPOWERED RUNNER

And if the Spirit of him who raised Jesus from the dead is living in you, he who raised Christ from the dead will also give life to your mortal bodies because of his Spirit who lives in you. (Romans 8:11 NIV)

"Running is way too hard!" Step, step. "I want to quit." Step, step. "I really want to quit!" Step, step. "Okay, I really want to quit!" Sound familiar? For some reason, running can rock us to our very core, leaving us uncertain of taking even one more step!

Life can feel much the same way. Iffy and uncertain! But hold up! You are no ordinary runner; you are a child of God! That's right; you have the power of the Holy Spirit living inside of you! That's right! You! Feeling powerless and hopeless? You do not have to fear one moment more. You have the strength of God living inside of you and do not have to live in a state of hesitation anymore! Instead, we can run confidently forward with the assurance of God's peace and joy that no matter what might stand before you, you can confidently run forward!

JULY 9TH RUNNING EXHAUSTED

Look to the LORD and his strength; seek his face always. (1 Chronicles 16:11 NIV)

It is mid afternoon and you have just finished a long, hard day at work. You are tired. Physically worn out and mentally drained. Running seems like the worst possible idea right now! Propping your feet up on the sofa and gorging on your favorite comfort food sounds like a dream come true! But you did make a commitment. So you drag your tired feet to the floor, change out of your comfy house clothes and into your running gear. However, as you jog along, your tiredness melts away and is replaced by energy! Most people would reason that the run would only make you more tired. But as runners we know it is just the opposite! Our run makes us feel revived! Energized!

Spending time with God can feel much the same way after a strenuous day. Reading God's Word and opening our hearts and minds just sounds like work. But as Christians, we realize just the opposite! When we give our worn out and weary hearts and minds to God, He renews us and fills us with hope, joy, and peace! Find your strength in Christ!

JULY 10TH RUNNING TO SHARE YOUR HOPE

But in your hearts revere Christ as Lord. Always be prepared to give an answer to everyone who asks you to give the reason for the hope that you have. But do this with gentleness and respect, (1 Peter 3:15 NIV)

You run with hope! Did you know that? As a runner you hold ambitions that others hope to aspire to! You have overcome so many obstacles to run.

As Christians we have a hope, don't we? Our hope lies in Christ! Jesus is our all! Jesus is the answer for our joy! Therefore we can be proud to tell everyone our story. The reason for your smile! The more you share all that Christ has done in your life, the more glory and honor you give God. The honor He deserves. So be ready to tell each and every person the reason for your hope. Have the answer for your joy prepared and ready on your lips. Share with others the reason you run! May the joy you have in Christ, shine in and through you like a light, for the whole world to see!

JULY 11TH RUNNING DOWN THE MYTHS

"For, "Everyone who calls on the name of the Lord will be saved." (Romans 10:13 NIV)

You've heard them around town. The endless rumors about running! Such as; you have to run miles and miles every day or you have to be super skinny and ridiculously fit! But you know they are all lies! You can run just as you are, just as God created you to be!

We all believe or create excuses not only to get out of running, but to not follow Jesus! We convince ourselves that now just isn't the right time or that our past condemns us. But that is not true! Jesus calls us to come just as you are! God wants you no matter what you have done or where you have been! Everyone who calls on Jesus will be saved! God will take every piece of your broken and damaged heart and make it new!

JULY 12TH RUNNING PLUGGED IN

Now you are the body of Christ, and each one of you is a part of it. (1 Corinthians 12:27 NIV)

Get connected! Yes, most especially in your running! Do your homework within your area to find a local running group. Run with a community of runners and see not only how much you improve from the fellow camaraderie, but how you can make a positive impact on others for Jesus.

In the same way, it is as important for believers to be plugged into God's kingdom work! We are the church and Jesus calls each and every one of us to go and live for Him! God commands us to live out our faith. We are all given individual skills and a place God has called us to. That could mean serving, teaching, reaching, or just doing whatever God puts in your heart to do. So what are you called to do? What great treasures do you have in store when you discover the great joy of serving God? Don't just sit there, get busy! Find that sweet spot God has called you to serve in His church, community, or even globally! Get plugged in today!

JULY 13ᵀᴴ RACE NIGHT JITTERS

The night before Herod was to bring him to trial, Peter was sleeping between two soldiers, bound with two chains, and sentries stood guard at the entrance. (Acts 12:6 NIV)

The monumental day will be here in the morning! Woo-hoo! All those lengthy hours and grueling miles you faithfully logged will finally pay off! You have arrived at the race you have long trained and diligently prepared for! As the minutes tick away bringing you closer and closer to the colossal race, you become more and more excited, restless, and tense. As you lie awake the night before the race, eyes wide open, heart pounding, staring at the darkness; all you can think about is toeing the starting line. How will you ever sleep?

But Peter was facing a much more serious dilemma and what was he doing the night before his trial? Sleeping! Peter wasn't restlessly twirling his thumbs or staring up in the dark. We never have to fear. We never have to be worried or anxious about anything. Ever! So don't lose one more ounce of sleep! So no matter what you are facing tomorrow, tonight you can rest assured knowing that everything is resting in the hands of a perfect God who never sleeps!

JULY 14ᵀᴴ RUNNING TO THANK YOUR CREATOR

I will give thanks to the LORD because of his righteousness; I will sing the praises of the name of the LORD Most High. (Psalm 7:17 NIV)

Wait! Pause right where you are and don't run another step! Have you stopped and taken the time today to thank God for all He has done and continues to do in your life? Thank God for the cozy bed you woke up in, the comfortable shoes on your feet, the fresh air you are breathing, and your ability to run! Thank God for the precious time you get to spend in His amazing presence.

Today is the day to make a conscious decision to thank God for each and every blessing He has placed in your life. Every step you take should be one of overflowing gratitude! As you run, thank God for the neighbors you pass. Thank God for the chipper birds and the beautiful songs they sing. Thank God for the gorgeous trees overhead who graciously offer their shade in the heat of the day. Thank God for the sun above that happily offers its warmth and glow. Have a heart of thankfulness the minute your feet touch the ground!

JULY 15ᵀᴴ RUNNING UNDER FIRE

Dear friends, I urge you, as foreigners and exiles, to abstain from sinful desires, which wage war against your soul. (1 Peter 2:11 NIV)

Ahhh! Feeling crushed by the overwhelming pressure to win? Is the stress to succeed and to be the best you can be harder than actually running itself?

Are you living your life feeling much the same way? Is the weight of the world too heavy for your shoulders? As a whole, we as society, place such high emphasis on what we look like, how much we weigh, what our job is, what we wear, and what we own. At work, employees feel the strain to climb the ladder while at school classmates feel the importance of being the most popular. But we are living for Jesus, not for man! So it's high time we decided to shift away from the expectations of the world and live in a way that glorifies God! God is so much more concerned with what your heart looks like than with what you are wearing or what car you are driving! God wants your complete submission and total devotion! True beauty is found in the hearts of those who seek Jesus!

JULY 16ᵀᴴ RUNNING THE BLAME GAME

"For those who exalt themselves will be humbled, and those who humble themselves will be exalted." (Matthew 23:12 NIV)

"It's not my fault!" Sound familiar? Running may be a solo sport but somehow we point the blame on others when we perform less than par. We accuse our shortcomings on just about everything and everyone but ourselves! We shift the responsibility of our running failure off ourselves and put the blame on everything from the roaring wind, the blazing sun, to the aggressive person running beside us.

Who are you pinning the blame on for your lack of time spent with God? Are you accusing someone or something else on your lack of seeking God? Instead of pride fully pointing your finger at others it is important to humble ourselves and turn that finger in the right direction, towards ourselves! Seek God with all your heart, soul, and mind and live your life in a way that glorifies God! Run hard! Giving God all the worship, glory, and honor He deserves!

JULY 17TH ACHY MUSCLES

"The greatest among you will be your servant." (Matthew 23:11 NIV)

So maybe you are feeling a little stiff. People at work are staring at you as you sway down the hallway like an old cowboy. Instead of smoothly sitting down into your office chair, you fall into your seat with a vicious plop, as you desperately grab at anything to break your fall. Let's not even talk about taking the stairs! Elevator please! Even though you can barely walk you don't really seem to mind. Your stiff and nagging muscles are a runner's badge of honor. A triumphant trophy you should be proud of! You are a literal walking gold medal reminder of all the strain and toil you put into your run. You gave it your all and you left nothing behind. You can literally feel a sense of accomplishment because you know you are only getting stronger and maturing as a runner.

Do you feel the growing pains of your Christian journey? Jesus calls us to serve and to be the hands and feet of Christ. Challenge yourself to find new ways to serve others, even though you are busy and tired. Unselfishly doing things for others in need has a special way of rejuvenating you. So put those "serving muscles" to good use!

JULY 18TH DIRTY FEET

"Now that I, your Lord and Teacher, have washed your feet, you also should wash one another's feet. I have set you an example that you should do as I have done for you." (John 13:14-15 NIV)

There's thick, slimy mud everywhere, literally! From your head all the way down to your toes. Your shoes are caked with the soft, sticky sludge that holds tight between the tread and decorates the laces. You just got done running through the muck and the mud, having the absolute time of your life!

The evidence of your shoes points to a romp in the wet woods but do your hands and feet point to serving others for Christ in the streets? Do your feet prove you have been busy sharing the gospel? Do your hands bear the marks of helping others? Our hands and feet give us away don't they? They show if we have been using our talents and time to show others the love of Christ that is in us. So get busy! Get your hands and feet grimy! It's time to get down, get dirty, and start joyfully serving our Savior and King.

JULY 19TH RUNNING REFLECTIONS

I seek you with all my heart; do not let me stray from your commands. I have hidden your word in my heart that I might not sin against you. (Psalm 119:10-11 NIV)

Who's that? Wait, that's you! That's your reflection in the gym mirror, all rosy cheeked and sweating hard on the treadmill. Hey, you are looking good! Mirrors, throughout the gym, show the runner's form and reveal the athlete's strengths, as well as their weaknesses.

Like a mirror, the Bible is revealing. God calls us to live a life that is holy and set apart, and the Bible shows us just how to do just that! But how do you know what's inside until you check it out? So open your Bible and dig in. The Bible is true, alive, and accurate. It is there to guide our way, every step we take!

JULY 20TH RUNNING CHAMPION

And let us consider how we spur one another on toward love and good deeds, not giving up meeting together, as some are in the habit of doing, but encouraging one another-and all the more as you see the Day approaching. (Hebrews 10:24-25 NIV)

Getting the gold isn't the only way to be a champion. The most blessed way to win is to be a blessing to others. So, how can you do that?

Be a running champion today! Be someone who uplifts and rallies beside others. Be an advocate and a voice of inspiration for those who run beside you! Everyone needs motivation, a loving nudge when life gets rocky and disheartening.

As a runner, there are so many people you can run alongside, lovingly cheering them on to achieve and accomplish their treasured goal. As believers, we must strive to support and spur one another on to live lives that glorify God. We all need some whoops and hurrahs, a warm hug, or a note of encouragement to fire up our lives for Christ! Be a flame of God's love, lighting the way to Christ for all to see! Brighten someone else's day with the light that shines in you.

JULY 21ST RUNNING LIKE A CHILD OF GOD

So in Christ Jesus you are all children of God through faith, (Galatians 3:26 NIV)

Did you know that when you accept Jesus as your Lord and Savior, you become a child of God? As a child of God, our son and daughter-ship arrives hand-in-hand with some really awesome gifts, such as; forgiveness, love, mercy, grace, hope, and freedom, just to name a few. Most importantly as a child of God we are promised an eternal life with our Father in heaven. Isn't that wonderful? You are a child of God! So while you are out running today, turn this idea over and over in your head. What does being a daughter or a son of God mean to you? What does it look like and how does it change how you run, act, and live?

JULY 22ND I'M A RUNNER INSIDE AND OUT

Create in me a pure heart, O God, and renew a steadfast spirit within me. (Psalm 51:10 NIV)

Yep, you can see it! You are a runner inside and out! You are a runner to the core. You know what else? You are beautiful to the core! You are beautiful just how you are, just as your Heavenly Father created you to be!

As a follower of Jesus, you were changed from the inside out! A total life saving transformation has taken place, you have a new heart! That means that the fire that everyone sees shining from you is just an overflowing light from the love of Jesus inside you! The things you say and the things you do originate from the outpouring of appreciation of the mercy, grace, and forgiveness God has generously showered on you! So run in a way that everyone can see Jesus in you! Be a mirror, to reflect the love, God has shown you!

JULY 23RD RUNNING LIKE GOD IS FOR YOU!

What, then, shall we say in response to these things? If God is for us, who can be against us? (Romans 8:31 NIV)

The wind might be against you, literally! Your body might want to take a break, truly! The sun's heat might be daring you to quit, actually! Other runners might be faster, really! Even your own family and friends might convince you otherwise, truly! Everything in running can seem to stand against you, but even knowing this, you can run with the assurance of one thing, God is for you!

So if God is for you, who dares stand against you? The answer is nothing! Nothing can stand in your way, not what others say, past mistakes, current struggles, and not even what you tell yourself! The God we serve is so powerful, so mighty, and so awesome that nothing and no one is greater than our God! Not even death could keep Jesus down! So if the God you serve cannot be held down, why are you letting anything hold you back from the person He created you to be?

JULY 24TH A RUNNER'S STORY

Jesus replied, "Very truly I tell you, no one can see the kingdom of God unless they are born again." (John 3:3 NIV)

Why did you start running? What drove you to jump off the blocks and race down the track to a new you? Every runner's story is unique, individual. Just like them! Some runners began running to lose weight, others to make a healthy life change, and still others were in searching to embark on a brand new adventure! However your running journey began, all runners can agree on one thing, running has changed you. You have become stronger inside and out!

You remember how you got your running start, but when did you make a decision to becoming a follower of Jesus? Have your testimony ready when someone asks you when or how you became saved. They may just ask what is different about you because they see a positive change in your life. The joy we find in Jesus is everlasting, undeniable, and flowing through you! So what's your story?

JULY 25TH RUNNING HOW?

Give praise to the LORD, proclaim his name; make known among the nations what he has done. (Psalm 105:1 NIV)

You are often reminded to keep in mind your running mechanics, to keep proper running posture, and to stay relaxed! How did running become harder than it already is!

Like getting caught up in the mechanics of running, have you ever gotten stuck in the "how" of evangelism? Confused by what tract to use, what approach to take, what to wear, what not to wear, what to bring, what not to bring, or how to even approach the topic? Sharing the gospel with biblical truth and accuracy is all that matters! When you approach someone with the love of Jesus in your heart, the details will seem to melt away and you will find the words to say and how to say them. God created us all uniquely. In your own special way you can spread the love of Jesus! So don't fret so much on the logistics and focus on the love of Christ you want to share.

JULY 26TH FOLLOWING JESUS

"Come, follow me," Jesus said, (Matthew 4:19a)

Hurry! Yep, it's time to grab your shoes and get going. Jesus is waiting for you! We are called to follow after our Savior! That's right, follow in the footsteps of our Messiah, everywhere He goes! Run close behind. You stay in the shadow of God's steps, always near Him because as you have learned, that when you let distance come between you and Him, it becomes harder and harder to follow.

We begin to lose sight, become distracted by the sights and sounds of our busy lives, and before you know it, we have lost sight of God altogether. But do not fear! God never left you! God was there the whole time, right beside you! So keep going! Stay strong. Finish the course following Jesus. Do as Jesus does. Say what Christ would have you say. Love as Jesus shows you how to love! Do not be afraid because you are following Jesus!

JULY 27TH RUNNING MINDSET

Finally, brothers and sisters, whatever is true, whatever is noble, whatever is right, whatever is pure, whatever is lovely, whatever is admirable-if anything is excellent or praiseworthy- think about such things. (Philippians 4:8 NIV)

Hold up! Stop running for a second. What were you just thinking about? Running stops and starts based on what thoughts the runner chooses to meditate on. We can either choose to concentrate on thoughts that motivate us or thoughts that slow us down. What drives you to propel to that next level? What motivates you continually run forward and dodge a negative mindset?

Okay, now in real time. What is your heart dwelling on? Which thoughts do you allow to take residence in your home: uplifting Christ-like positives or ugly negatives? Choose to focus on what is true, noble, right, pure, lovely, admirable, excellent, and praiseworthy! Dwell on such things as these not only while running but in whatever you do!

JULY 28TH PIZZA, PIES, AND PANCAKES

This is why it is said: "Wake up, sleeper, rise from the dead, and Christ will shine on you." (Ephesians 5:14 NIV)

Boxes of cheesy pizza, mounds of yummy cookies, and bags of mouth watering candy beckon you to sit and indulge! As runners we sometimes think that just because we run we are now entitled to all the fat, starches, sugars, and calories we desire.

Just like giving yourself a free pass at the dinner table, are you giving yourself a free pass in life just because you know you are saved? But now is not the time to sit back and enjoy, but to get busy and on the move for God's glory! Let's rock and roll! Our lives are not our own but God's. To live in a way that pleases and glorifies our King!

JULY 29ᵀᴴ RUNNING SHORT

For all have sinned and fall short of the glory of God, and all are justified freely by his grace through the redemption that came by Christ Jesus. (Romans 3:23-24 NIV)

Falling short? Missing the mark by just a smidge? You train hard, eat well, stick to your plan, but still feel like you are falling just shy of your goal or how fast you could be!

We often fall short in life too don't we? We fall just below passing, we miss that deadline by just a day, or we get passed up for that amazing promotion that we had been working so hard for. As a human race, we have all missed the mark. Every single one of us! We have all sinned and fallen short. All of us! But do not be afraid! That is not where the story ends! Jesus came so that we may have life! Our one and only hope can be found in Christ Jesus and in His death and resurrection. It is in Jesus we have the promise of eternal life! This gift is only given through faith in Jesus. Jesus is the only way!

JULY 30ᵀᴴ DOUBLE KNOT THEN RUN

"But when you pray, go into your room, close the door and pray to your Father, who is unseen. Then your Father, who sees what is done in secret, will reward you." (Matthew 6:6 NIV)

Loop one bunny ear through the other bunny ear, pull, and knot it twice! Do you take that extra moment to double knot your shoes? By double tying you minimize the risk of having to stop and take the time to re-tie loose ends while running, better yet, during a race!

Okay, double knotting might seem so ridiculously simple it is not even worth mentioning, but so much of what we view as "trivial" and "small" matter the most! In our lives it can be so easy to overlook quiet, quality time with our Heavenly Father. Time spent in God's glorious presence, opening your ears and yielding your heart to Him. Spending time with God should never be underestimated, every precious minute with our Savior counts! Take the time to discover all that God wants to share with you!

JULY 31ˢᵀ RUN LIKE THE BEST

But just as he who called you is holy, so be holy in all you do; for it is written: Be holy, because I am holy." (1 Peter 1:15-16 NIV)

Keep going! You can do it! Never give up! Reach for those stars. You can do even more than you could ever imagine when you do it through Christ who gives us strength! God gave us the perfect example to live after. Jesus! The perfect Son of God.

When you run for Jesus, Jesus will be seen living through you. Jesus will be revealed in you for all to see! We live to be conformed to God's image.

"We always carry around in our body the death of Jesus, so that the life of Jesus may also be revealed in our body." (2 Corinthians 4:10 NIV)

So run like the best because you are following the best. Jesus can be seen in you and in everything you do when you live for Him! Stay close to Jesus, for His love endures forever!

AUGUST 1ˢᵀ NOT READY TO RUN!

"But the Advocate, the Holy Spirit, whom the Father will send in my name, will teach you all things and will remind you of everything I have said to you." (John 14:26 NIV)

You literally feel like the asphalt is melting beneath your feet. You desperately lick your lips as the sun beats unabashedly on your exposed head. Not only did you forget your water bottle but you forgot your sunscreen, hat, sunglasses, and shorts! You started your run in the crisp morning air and now feel the heat of a quickly rising summer's sun! Running unprepared is never pleasant, especially when you forget the essential things that make running easier!

In life it can be easy to feel unprepared, especially when telling someone else about Jesus. You feel ready, you pray that God would bring someone in your life to tell, but when the big moment comes, you choke! You go home dismayed and question how God can ever use you. But do not fret! Do not fear! It is not your words but God's! You do not have to be afraid because the Holy Spirit is residing within you, He will give you the words to say! All you have to be is willing to be used as a voice for those precious words of salvation to be transported through! So even if you feel unprepared and a little perplexed, step your toes out in faith, the Holy Spirit will be there to guide you!

AUGUST 2ND A SEASIDE RUN

The heavens declare the glory of God; the skies proclaim the work of his hands. (Psalm 19:1 NIV)

Whoosh! Splash! The ocean waves kiss your ankles and then hurriedly melt away back into the ocean. The squawky song of seagulls can be heard from above. Ah! What a breathtaking experience! Running near the ocean or beside the lakeshore is quite an experience for any runner. As you attempt to avoid the unrelenting waves while feeling the energy of a constantly moving body of water is an awesome experience.

Running along the warm sand and looking out on that dark blue span of water makes it abundantly easy to appreciate not only the beauty of God's creation but of His power. It is easy to feel just how small we are compared to the vastness of God's creation. Take the time to appreciate the work of God's creation and all that His hands have made. Everything our eyes behold is because God made it and because He saw it as good. So as you run today breathe in and out, thankful to serve such a powerful Creator.

AUGUST 3RD RUNNING OH SO GOOD

But whose delight is in the law of the LORD, and who meditates on his law day and night. That person is like a tree planted by streams of water, which yields its fruit in season and whose leaf does not wither- whatever they do prospers. (Psalm 1:2-3 NIV)

Do you know that point in your run when running just feels effortless, easy as pie? Although this only happens every so often, the joy of this run is memorable. It is so freeing and enjoyable to find that sweet spot in your run!

Even better than finding your happiness in your run, is falling in love with Jesus, a happiness that brings pure joy to those who faithfully trust Him! You seek God because you love Him. You trust God because He is faithful. You depend on God because He is proven trustworthy. It's time for more Jesus in your life! Make the decision to want more of God in every moment of every day. Joyfully serve God, seek Him, and fall head over heels in love with your Messiah!

AUGUST 4TH ONE SWEATY RUN

But the eyes of the LORD are on those who fear him, on those whose hope is in his unfailing love, (Psalm 33:18 NIV)

Envision this: you are running down the sidewalk under a sizzling summer sun. Not a hopeful cloud can be found in the bright blue sky. Your feet pound heavily against the pavement. Sweat begins to pour down your already damp forehead and lazily trickles into your eyes. Immediately you feel the perspiration start to irritate your eyes and you begin to have a distorted vision of the sidewalk ahead!

Like the distorted view of sweat in your eyes, is your vision blurred when it comes to life on earth? As a Christian is it easy to live as our society does, instead of how we know we are called to live. God's way is opposite of how our culture tempts us to live. Humanity tells us to live for ourselves; Jesus calls us to live humbly, as a servant. Humankind tells us that to be happy we have to own a big house, a nice car, and lots of money. Jesus tells us to store up our treasures in heaven. It is so easy for our vision to become hazy and to become confused on what's really important, but remember when we fix your eyes on Jesus, our focus becomes clear!

AUGUST 5TH FEET OF JOY

Though you have not seen him, you love him; and even though you do not see him now, you believe in him and are filled with an inexpressible and glorious joy, (1 Peter 1:8 NIV)

Have you ever felt like your attitude toward running was contingent on how your "running life" was going? When you are running fast and easily, running makes you smile. However, once an injury strikes or the training becomes too hard, your smile quickly gets turned upside down! It is easy to have a love/hate relationship with running. Quite honestly it is easy to feel that way about just about anything in life. When things are going good we are satisfied but once they turn ugly…watch out!

But with Jesus, things are different, in a glorious way! We might be happy one day and sad the next, sure. However, as believers we have a special weapon! Joy! An everlasting joy can only comes from accepting Jesus as your Lord and Savior. As God's children we can have an unending joy that will allow us to face any and all circumstances. That joy is only found through Christ! Only in Jesus can true joy be found!

AUGUST 6TH RUNNING OVERWHELMED

But this happened that we might not rely on ourselves but on God, who raises the dead. (2 Corinthians 1:9b NIV)

A wave of anxiety washed over you. You feel utterly overwhelmed. As you look to your right and to your left, all you see is a sea of unending colors. You can literally feel the pulses of excitement from the runners standing beside you. You look straight. You swallow hard. You begin to ask yourself "how".

"How are you going to run all those miles?"

Life can be overwhelming just like running can be! Every day we not only face, but can be easily overcome with feelings of inadequacy, doubt, fear, distractions, un-forgiveness, guilt, anger, and that list could go on and on. It is important that when we feel this way to bring our overwhelming feelings, things, and problems to God! The sooner and the faster we give God our "overwhelmings", the quicker we can face whatever it is, hand in hand, with Him! Our God is a God who is all powerful, He created the Earth, with Him nothing is impossible!

AUGUST 7TH RUN THE DATE...

"Very truly I tell you, whoever hears my word and believes him who sent me has eternal life and will not be judged but has crossed over from death to life." (John 5:24 NIV)

Okay think back. Way back! Turn back the clock by breaking out your old calendar. Do you remember the date when you started your running journey? Whatever the reason, whatever the age, congratulations on becoming a runner! Look how far you have come since that memorable day!

In the same way, do you remember when you became a Christian? Do you recall when you made the decision to trust Jesus as your Lord and Savior? You are a new creation! Your sins are covered by the redeeming blood of Jesus and that calls for celebration! Share your life changing experience with someone today. Tell them all that Jesus has done and continues to do in your new life! Share the love of our Messiah with a friend, a colleague, or your neighbor. Let the whole world know how much God loves them!

AUGUST 8TH WILL YOU RUN WITH ME?

Glorify the LORD with me; let us exalt his name together. (Psalm 34:3 NIV)

Close your eyes. Now think of one person you know who you could ask to run with you. Now open your eyes! Who was it that you thought of? Not everyone wants to run, but maybe there is someone in your life who would love to exercise with you or is just looking for that little extra push to get started. Will you be the encouragement that friend needs?

So now you have someone to run with but who do you know that might just be waiting for that invitation to go with you to church? Take those two names you have in your head and do something about it! Ask God to give you the courage and strength to be the vessel used to spread His love. Boldly ask others to join you in your race for Jesus!

AUGUST 9TH REST DAY

Then God blessed the seventh day and made it holy, because on it he rested from all the work of creating that he had done. (Genesis 2:3 NIV)

Whew! It's time to get those feet up take a rest today! You have been faithfully logging the miles all week long and now it is time to take a well earned break from all your hard work. Rest days are crucial for becoming a successful runner! We need to give our muscles and bodies a well deserved break.

God in his infinite wisdom created a day of rest. God created the heavens and the earth in six day and on the seventh He rested. Our Creator set the seventh day apart, making it holy and a very special day. We are also called to honor the Sabbath and honor our Heavenly Father on this special day. So take rest from your labor in His presence today, thanking God for all He has done!

AUGUST 10TH RUNNING FOCUSED

Being strengthened with all power according to his glorious might so that you may have great endurance and patience, (Colossians 1:11 NIV)

Are you focused on your training? As a runner, are you inspired and motivated to achieve your goal? Staying focused means you keep your goal in mind as motivation to getting those miles in! When you love Jesus it is easy to want to live for Him! Why would you not want to? Jesus loves you, saved you, and continues to take care of and bless you every day! Time with Jesus should be cherished, never just endured. It's a relationship! We should consider ourselves blessed to be serving such an amazing Savior! Stay focused on what God is calling you to do!

AUGUST 11TH RUNNING LIKE THE STARS

Do everything without grumbling or arguing, so that you may become blameless and pure, "children of God without fault in a warped and crooked generation."

Then you shine among them like stars in the sky as you hold firmly to the word of life. And then I will be able to boast on the day of Christ that I did not run or labor in vain. (Philippians 2:14-16 NIV)

Do you find joy in running? This is not a trick question! If you answered no (and quite understandably) it's time to turn that no upside down! Unfortunately there is nothing we can do to remove the "run" from running. Running will always require hard work and sweat. However, there is something that can be changed. You!

So how do we start? Just Like everything else in life, it begins with your attitude! Your attitude can be the instrument of change that puts the joy into your run. Instead of grumbling and complaining about running, your job, your finances, your boss, and your family; it's time to remember the one thing you do have control of. Yourself! Bring a godly attitude and Christ-like joy to everything in your life and it will be a game changer! So enthusiastically charge forward in a way that brings God honor today! Be a shining star for Jesus, pointing towards Him for all to see!

AUGUST 12TH RUNNING TOWARDS THE GOLD

"Provide purses for yourselves that will not wear out, a treasure in heaven that will never fail, where no thief comes near and no moth destroys." (Luke 12:33b NIV)

The winner's medallion draped over a victorious runner's neck marking the accomplishment of a lifetime! To the runner, that gold circle means so much more than a decoration, but celebrates their courageous hard work, inspiring endurance, loving dedication, and their bold commitment.

Where is your cherished treasure? Is your heart's desire here on Earth, focused on things of this world or on treasures above? Make God your treasure chest. Make God the reason you do everything and anything. May the love to which you show others only be from the outpouring of love that you have for God. Be the love of Jesus here on earth showing mercy, compassion, and love to those all around you. Praise and glorify God using the talents and skills He has blessed you with. Run with your eyes on Jesus, the true treasure of your heart!

AUGUST 13TH RUNNERS STINK

May I never boast except in the cross of our Lord Jesus Christ, through which the world has been crucified to me, and I to the world. (Galatians 6:14 NIV)

Sniff, sniff, sniff… hey, what's that smell? When you run, you probably sweat, and when you sweat, you probably stink. Only a guess! Ever get a whiff of your workout clothes after a hard run or even worse, your socks and shoes? Phew! You can deny it if you want to but they probably do not smell like the fresh scent of candles!

Our attitudes, like our shoes, can also have a real smell to them! It is important to do an attitude check once in a while to keep a heart that is real, soft, and open! A heart that is moldable in God's hands. How has your attitude been at work, at school, toward your spouse, toward your co-worker, or towards strangers? Do you turn up your nose to strangers as you run by or have you been treating others with the same love God has graciously shown you? Ask God to open your eyes to see others as He does!

AUGUST 14TH RUNNING LOUD AND PROUD

Declare his glory among the nations, his marvelous deeds among all peoples. (Psalm 96:3 NIV)

"Running this" and "running that". You cannot help but gab about running to anyone and everyone! Given enough time and an available ear you probably could ramble on and on about running all day long!

But how much do you share about Jesus? Do you speak about Jesus to anyone and everyone you meet with the same passion and excitement you hold for running? You don't have to tell others about Jesus, you get to! How can you contain the love of Jesus who gave His very life for you! That's why it is the good news! It's good news to the soul that is hurting, lost, and broken. The story of our Savior is like balm to a heart that is seeking healing. So today you can feel blessed to be the privileged feet that are used to go and the lucky mouth that is used to proclaim the greatest story of all time!

AUGUST 15TH RUN IN THE NOW

"Therefore do not worry about tomorrow, for tomorrow will worry about itself. Each day has enough trouble of its own." (Matthew 6:34 NIV)

Busy, busy, busy bees! Runners shuffle around an already hectic schedule, yet still manage to somehow fit running into the mix! Our days, weeks, and months are full to the brim! We can become so focused on all that we have to do and all the places we have to be that we lose sight of the very day we are standing in! As runners we do this all the time! Instead of enjoying each and every moment that our feet are currently trekking through, we let our minds focus and even worry on the distant tomorrow.

So today, let's choose to live within today. To live life in the very moment that we are blessed with and rejoice in the time we are given by our Heavenly Father. Enjoy today's run, every step of it, instead of worrying about tomorrow's worries! Let us be present in the present, because today is a gift from God!

AUGUST 16TH ALL THE PLACES I LOVE TO RUN!

"Yours, LORD, is the greatness and the power and the glory and the majesty and the splendor, for everything that in heaven and earth is yours." (1 Chronicles 29:11a NIV)

Do you have a favorite place to run? That go-to-spot that promises to uplift your spirits, a place that reminds you of just how beautiful the world around you truly is! Maybe this perfect setting is where the golden sand meets the rolling waves or within the peaceful tranquility of a soft gravel trail winding through fresh whispering pines.

Where is your favorite place to meet with your Heavenly Father? Is your quintessential place at the breakfast nook where you eagerly meet the Almighty over steamy coffee, or maybe it's under the shade of an oak tree during lunch, perhaps it is within the quiet of a spare room on a wooden floor while on your knees. The physical setting does not matter so much as that you seek to be with God! So pick that favorite spot and open your ears, eyes, and heart to God's love! Your Heavenly Father is waiting to meet with you today!

AUGUST 17TH JUST LEAVE RUNNING TO THE PROS

Each of you should use whatever gift you have received to serve others, as faithful stewards of God's grace in its various forms. (1 Peter 4:10 NIV)

Whoa! Look at them go! Their legs are merely a blur! Watching the top elite race can leave anyone watching a bit awestruck. You are left scratching your head, how do they run so fast? But just because they are lightening fast doesn't mean you cannot run your very best, no matter what the speed! On the contrary, their extreme speed only inspires and invigorates you! Professional runners are not the only ones leaving us a bit speechless and totally star-struck!

In church, we are surrounded by remarkably talented brothers and sisters. Amongst so much aptitude and expertise, we begin to question if God can even use us! We begin to wonder if we should just leave God's work to the professionals. But hold up! You are just as important and as special in God's eyes. We are as equally accountable with the gifts God has given us! Use those beautiful gifts and special talents He has uniquely given you to the best of your God given ability!

AUGUST 18ᵀᴴ RUNNING AGAINST THE WIND

"If you fear the LORD and serve and obey him and do not rebel against his commands, and if both you and the king who reigns over you follow the LORD your God - good! But if you do not obey the LORD, and if you rebel against his commands, his hand will be against you, as it was against your ancestors." (1 Samuel 12:14-15 NIV)

Whoosh! The blustery wind wildly blows against your face. You swing your arms and aggressively pump your legs as hard as you can to reach the street corner that marks your turn around. Ah! You made it! That's so much better. Now with the wind to your back, you set sail, and almost fly home!

Following and obeying God is much like running with the wind. When we obediently follow God and seek His will, the joy of following Him blesses us through life. This does not necessarily mean that our way will be easier, quite the contrary! The Christian road is marked by many trials and tribulations. However, as followers of Jesus, we have an unending flow of joy that only comes from trusting Him every step the way!

AUGUST 19ᵀᴴ DAILY RUNNING WITH JESUS

Then he said to them all: "Whoever wants to be my disciple must deny themselves and take up their cross daily and follow me." (Luke 9:23 NIV)

No one becomes fit overnight. Nope, not even if you sleep beside your treadmill! To improve as a runner, you have to hit the grind every day, rain or shine.

Following Jesus is the same way! Being a faithful disciple of Jesus leaves no wiggle room for partial commitment. We need to be all in! Radically committed! Jesus requires a total commitment from us! Following and obeying Jesus requires a total transformation of our heart, self, time, and how we use blessings He has bestowed upon us! Are you committed to Jesus? Make being Christ's disciple an everyday top priority! Give Jesus every joyful moment and every precious second you are graciously given! Be all in, crazily in love, and joyfully following our Messiah's footsteps!

AUGUST 20TH MY BIRTHDAY RUN

"Before I formed you in the womb I knew you, before you were born I set you apart; I appointed you as a prophet to the nations." (Jeremiah 1:5 NIV)

Blow out the candles! Make a wish! If today is not your birthday, save this devotion for your special day! Your birthday is a noteworthy day and the perfect reason to celebrate! Today is a day to thank God for all He has done and continues to do in your life. Thank God for one more year He has given you on this earth. Thank God that you are a runner. Thank God that you have the ability to run each and every day to your heart's content!

As you work out today, thank your Creator for each and every step. You are blessed and a chosen child of God. Jesus loves you. By Christ's blood you are saved. Thank God for calling you to be a daughter or son of the one true King!

AUGUST 21ST RUNNING WEIGHTLESS

Cast all your anxiety on him because he cares for you. (1 Peter 5:7 NIV)

Rattle, rattle, clunk, clunk! Any guess on what that sound is? That sound is you running! You nosily run around with your keys, sunglasses, cell phone, headphones, fuel belt, water, nutrition, and your music! All this extra luggage can make a runner feel more like a pack animal than a nimble footed winner! Maybe it isn't running that is leaving you tired but the backbreaking emotional baggage you are carrying around.

Guilt, fear, anxiety, a life altering diagnosis, hurt, loss, troubles, financial weight, pain, loss of a loved one; all these heavy things can leave you feeling exhausted, alone, and discouraged. The great news? You don't have to tediously carry these cumbersome cares anymore! You can lay your burdens down at God's feet while He holds you in His loving arms. Those things are just too heavy to carry around anymore! Only through Jesus can we run lighter, freer, and more joyfully!

AUGUST 22ND RUNNING LOST

We all, like sheep, have gone astray, each of us has turned to our own way; and the LORD has laid on him the iniquity of us all. (Isaiah 53:6 NIV)

Wait a second; did you take a wrong turn somewhere? You were running along a familiar route but must have taken the incorrect road somewhere along the way. Anxiety starts to creep in. You ask yourself, "Where are you?"

We were all at one time separated from God. We all ran down our own road and took our own way. We were lost in our sin and disconnected from God. But that's where the story begins! Jesus Christ, the sinless Son of God, died on the cross for the sins of the whole world! Isn't that amazing! Jesus bridged the gap that once separated us from God and through faith in Jesus we have the promise of eternal life! So you are no longer running around lost and adrift, but found! You were once searching in the dark and now you are shining in the light of Christ!

AUGUST 23ᴿᴰ MY RUNNING JOURNEY

So then, just as you received Christ Jesus as Lord, continue to live your lives in him, rooted and built up in him, strengthened in the faith as you were taught, and overflowing with thankfulness. (Colossians 2:6-7 NIV)

When you start running, you embark on a road trip, a journey to become the very best runner you can be! This is much easier said than done! Running requires you to work hard, train smart, and stick to your schedule to become the best possible running you can be!

As Christians we are called to follow a perfect Savior. As humans, this is not so simple! When we become a believer, we don't just arrive; we must become increasingly more and more like Christ. This beautiful and blessed voyage starts once when we accept Jesus as our Lord and Savior and continues until the day we see our Savior in heaven!

AUGUST 24ᵀᴴ BELIEVE

Then he said to Thomas, "Put your finger here; see my hands. Reach out your hand and put it into my side. Stop doubting and believe." (John 20:27 NIV)

You can handle this! You can do this! No sweat. Okay, maybe a little! You can finish the daunting race that lies before you! You can make it! Believe in yourself! You are strong inside and out! Confidently run the race before you with boldness and courage.

You know who else believes in you? God! Yes, that's right He believes in you! God is right beside you, there to strengthen and help you, every step of the way! God wants you to succeed. Your Maker has even given you the tools and skills to do it! Whatever you do, do it with all of your heart, and with everything you are! Give God your very best, your all! In everything you do, glorify God. Live for God, always giving Him your very best! Believe in yourself because the creator of the universe believes in you and desires you to succeed!

AUGUST 25ᵀᴴ RUNNING WITH ADMIRATION

Praise the LORD, my soul; all my inmost being, praise his holy name. (Psalm 103:1 NIV)

Make your running a worshipful experience! Focus your heart, mind, and footsteps on praising our Everlasting King! Lift up each foot in admiration for all the things God has done and continues to do. With each step you take, meditate on God's grace and goodness.

"My mouth is filled with your praise, declaring your splendor all day long." (Psalm 71:8 NIV)

Redirect every thought of worry and fear into one that glorifies our Father in heaven. Focus on how great our God truly is! Dedicate your heart and your run to God! Today is the best day to practice a heart of thankfulness. As you strap on your running shoes, prepare and tune your heart to focus on all that God is! Inhale and exhale thoughts of God's gratefulness and love. You are a chosen child of God! That's all the reason in the world to run thankful!

AUGUST 26ᵀᴴ AND THEY'RE OFF!

After this the Lord appointed seventy-two others and sent them two by two ahead of him to every town and place where he was about to go. (Luke 10:1 NIV)

Picture this: hundreds of runners lining up in the coolness of the morning. Their eyes are focused straight ahead, with hope, expectancy and excitement racing through their bodies. You can see their nervous breath hanging in the air. You can feel the electricity all around you. The front row toes the line. Boom! The loud crack of the starting gun pierces the silence and they're off! If you have run a race you can relate to the anxiety and butterflies related to the starting line. It is hard not to be excited; there is a wide open race in front of you waiting to be conquered!

Like a runner toeing the line, you are about to be sent off! God is calling you to use the talents and gifts He has given you to glorify Him! Where is God sending you? Is God sending you to the neighbor next door or across the world? Are you excited? Are you ready?

AUGUST 27ᵀᴴ RUNNING TO MY HEART'S DESIRE

Take delight in the LORD, and he will give you the desires of your heart. (Psalm 37:4 NIV)

What do you need to become a great runner? Only one thing: Desire! You can run on grass, sand, on the road, on a quiet trail in the middle of the woods, inside or out, in the pouring rain, or on a crisp sunny day. You can do it literally almost anywhere and at anytime. Nothing can stop you! All you need is a heart that wants to run.

As a believer of Jesus, no materials are required to follow Him. None! Only faith in Jesus Christ is required and faith in Him alone. The great news is that we can spread the good news anywhere and everywhere! We can be Christ's disciples at work, at home, running on the street, at the gym, in the store, or in the post office. We can preach God's Word in our own community, on a mission trip, or even on your vacation! The opportunities are endless! So run for Jesus to your heart's desire, faithfully spreading the love of Jesus along the way!

AUGUST 28ᵀᴴ RUNNING IN A FRACTURED WORLD

For as in Adam all die, so in Christ all will be made alive. (1 Corinthians 15:22 NIV)

Runners are fragile. Delicate. We are easily broken and susceptible to any and all injuries. We are literally just one step away from a break, a bruise, or a tear. One second from losing the race. But our frailty is not unique to just runners, but is common to all humans as a whole.

We live in a broken, bruised, and fractured world because of sin. By God's standards we all deserve eternal death. Every single one of us! Okay, so now for the good news! Through faith in Jesus we have life, everlasting life! We are no longer enslaved to sin and death but have life through The One who took our place! Thank you Jesus! Life can be scary, even uncertain. Just remember we never have to live that way! We can live boldly and confidently through Christ who saved us! Live strong! Run strong!

AUGUST 29ᵀᴴ RUNNERS, TRUST THE SOURCE

"Sanctify them by the truth; your word is truth." (John 17:17 NIV)

To become a better runner, we run. Instead of sitting on the sidelines and watching others pass us by, we jump in and put our shoes to the pavement. But how often do we solely depend on others to tell us what is in the Bible instead of opening God's Word and discovering what's inside for ourselves!

The Bible is alive! Scripture is the living truth that is open and ready for us to uncover the love, mercy, and goodness of God for ourselves! Within, its pages, we unveil the life saving story of God's forgiveness and grace extended to us all. So please listen to your pastor, your small group leader, and your grandmother, but do not let your dependency for spiritual maturation end there! Go straight to the source! God is waiting to speak to you. Are you ready to read and listen?

AUGUST 30TH RUNNING IN COLOR

In the beginning God created the heavens and the earth. (Genesis 1:1 NIV)

The colors of God's creation are all around. Surrounding you like an amazing painted canvass. As your beautiful feet travel down the speckled trail you are overcome by the beauty of God's portrait of shades. Above you lies the breathtaking blues of the sky highlighted by white fluffy clouds. Around the trail grows the greens of God's grasses and leaves. The yellow of the sun shines high above the whites of the clouds while the purples of God's flowers peek above the grassy greens.

Ah, take time to appreciate all the artwork of God's creation! The earth is our Maker's handiwork and everything in it! God holds the paintbrush, the world is His easel, and you are His creation. You are the Almighty's treasured child. We are the clay in God's hands, lovingly being molded and shaped!

AUGUST 31ST RUNNING STRONG IN THE LORD

He gives strength to the weary and increases the power of the weak. Even youths grow tired and weary, and young men stumble and fall; but those who hope in the LORD will renew their strength. They will soar on wings like eagles; they will run and not grow weary, they will walk and not be faint. (Isaiah 40:29-31 NIV)

Ahead of you looms the long, hilly, winding road. The heat of the summer day sizzles like a fajita off the stove. But you are not daunted, you are by no means scared! You have not only the courage but the strength to fly through this workout! Sure it's hot out, sure you do not feel like running, but this is nothing, you can do it!

Do you need a source of strength today? Strength to get through whatever life is throwing your way? As Christians we have an overflowing, powerful, and everlasting source of strength. God is our strength! Jesus is our rock, and fortress, and our salvation. Those who hope in Him will discover their strength in the Lord. They will run and not grow weary! Let us soar with wings like eagles, trusting in the Almighty's arms!

SEPTEMBER 1ST FEET OFF THE GROUND

But our citizenship is in heaven. And we eagerly await a Savior from there, the Lord Jesus Christ, (Philippians 3:20 NIV)

As believers, we are not running for blue we are running for red! Instead of running for the trophies and awards of the world or the accomplishments of yourself, we victoriously run forward covered and redeemed by the red blood of Jesus Christ. We run for the red of love, because we have already won the blue in Christ. We no longer run for ourselves but for Jesus!

We run out of the outpouring of love we have for God! Because of God's love, we run forward in eager expectation to share the good news of salvation with each and every person our feet encounter. So our feet might be running on the ground, but our hearts are set on heaven! Run for God always, for God alone.

"Sitting down, Jesus called the Twelve and said, "Anyone wants to be first must be the very last, and the servant of all.""" (Mark 9:35 NIV)

SEPTEMBER 2ND FREE TO RUN

"So if the Son sets you free, you will be free indeed" (John 8:36 NIV)

Have you ever miserably failed a race? So often we allow a past negative event dictate our future. We are so focused on our failures that we lose sight of what lies ahead of us. As runners we can beat ourselves up at times.

Past negative experiences in life do much the same thing. We just cannot let them go. We refuse to forgive ourselves. So we sit and dwell on it, all the time, night and day. The good news? The moment you ask for forgiveness, God forgives. Boom, the sin is removed. Just like that. So if Jesus is not holding your sins against you, why are you? Your sins were nailed once and for all to the cross, there is no reason to continue to pound yourself for actions that you have already been forgiven. Let it go today! It's never too late! Let go of your guilt and freely run forward with a grateful heart!

SEPTEMBER 3RD A LABOR OF LOVE

Whatever you do, work at it with all your heart, as working for the Lord, not for human masters, (Colossians 3:23 NIV)

Today is your day all you hard workers! Today is a day of celebration in honor of whatever it is your hands and feet have found joy in doing! God wants to use you and whatever it is that you do to glorify Him! That literally means whatever you do, do it for God! God wants to use your skills and your talents to honor Him right from where you are.

So glorify God all you farmers from your fields, teachers glorify God from your classrooms, moms and dads glorify God from your house, glorify God all you construction men and women from your scaffolds, pilots glorify God from your planes, nurses glorify God from your bedsides, fireman glorify God from your ladders, and glorify God lineman from your electric poles. Whatever you do, do it with all your heart and with everything you are, for The One who created You! That means, you runners, yes you! Run in a way that glorifies God! May every step you take be taken in a way that honors God Almighty!

SEPTEMBER 4TH YOUR RUNNING POTENTIAL

I pray that the eyes of your heart may be enlightened in order that you may know the hope to which he has called you, the riches of his glorious inheritance in his holy people, (Ephesians 1:18 NIV)

You stop. You are totally out of breath and utterly tired! You have had enough of running for today, maybe even longer! The bad news? You can still see your driveway from where you now stand. You only ran a mile! The good news? You ran a whole mile! That mile is one half mile further than the half mile you said you would never be able to run! You have potential! Yes you! When you put your best efforts into action you can do whatever you put your mind to!

God has a great plan for you and your life and He has blessed you with unique skills and talents. You have the potential to make a difference in this world for God's glory! Isn't that amazing? You can do anything through Christ! So put some willpower, some strength, and some oomph into that potential! You have the raw skills; you just need to start putting them into use! Where can you be used? What can you do to praise, worship, and glorify a God that loved you so much that He sent His own Son to die in your place? What will you do with all your potential?

SEPTEMBER 5TH ENERGIZED TO RUN

LORD, be gracious to us; we long for you. Be our strength every morning, our salvation in time of distress. (Isaiah 33:2 NIV)

Ring! Ring! Ring! The persistent sound of your alarm announces the arrival of 5:00 A.M. The inviting silence of dark closes around you as you step onto the cold hardwood floor and quickly dress into your running wardrobe. After tying your shoes and heading out into the brisk morning chill, you turn onto the empty road ahead of you. Meanwhile the same thought spins around and round in your head, "Man I wish I could just stay in bed!"

Okay so maybe your running scenario plays out differently, but no matter what the synopsis, running requires expending energy to see it through. Energy that most non runners argue is better spent unused! However, you as a runner knows a secret. Running gives you energy! Seems kind of backwards right? So is spending time with God! Time spent in God's Word and in prayer only leaves us feeling re-energized, full of hope, and overflowing with joy. Spend time with Jesus to renew and rejuvenate your hungry soul!

SEPTEMBER 6TH RUNNING THANKFUL

Rejoice always, pray continually, give thanks in all circumstances; for this is God's will for you in Christ Jesus. (1 Thessalonians 5:16-18 NIV)

You made it. Whew! You blew that workout out of the water! Not only did you accomplish your run but you made it home safely, in one piece, injury free and maybe even with a smile! You are probably patting yourself on the back for a job well done but doesn't God deserve the true praise?

Thank God that gave you one more day to run! Thank God that that you now feel refreshed and reenergized to energetically tackle the rest of your day! Thank God for the loving net of safety and protection He delicately places over you. Thank God from the bottom of your heart and fill your prayers with true thanks-giving. Thank God for all those things we so often take for granted like a roof over your head, food on your plate, and a car in your driveway. When you begin to thank God for the smallest of blessings, your day will start to overflow with praise. Run with an eternally thankful heart!

SEPTEMBER 7TH RUNNING DECISIONS

I run in the path of your commands, for you have broadened my understanding. (Psalm 119:32 NIV)

It's Sunday morning. Twenty minutes until your group run. Originally your once a week group run was scheduled for Thursday nights, perfect for you. But then several of the runners had to miss because of various scheduling conflicts. At first running on Sundays was no big deal. Missing church isn't that bad... right? Uh oh! Has running (or anything else) consumed your life so much that nothing else matters?

Is something (other than God) on the top shelf of your life? It is imperative that we all ask ourselves if we hold anything above our devotion, our enthusiasm, and our adoration of our Heavenly Father! God desires to be our all and everything. Nothing, absolutely nothing, can be held higher than our God Almighty. So no matter what you do, do it for God. Remember to use your skills and talents to bring glory to our King. So when you run, run in a way that points others to His love and His mercy. Give God your all and ask that He would help you run in a way that bring honor to Him. Ask God to place others in your path today that you will be able to share with them the reason for your Joy!

SEPTEMBER 8TH STUCK AT A LIGHT

Wait for the LORD; be strong and take heart and wait for the LORD. (Psalm 27:14 NIV)

The traffic light quickly turns from a green to a cautious yellow to then stopping you safely on red. In your impatience, you wildly jog in place, anxious and ready to get running again. The longer you wait the more impatient you become with the stoplight. You have a lot to do today, but first you have a workout to finish!

Are you figuratively stopped at a red light in your everyday life? Do you feel like you are sitting on the sidelines while everyone else is happily playing the game? As you impatiently watch you begin to ask, "God when will you use me? Put me into the game! I want to be used!"

Waiting for God, is never easy. But know this, as you patiently wait to be used by God, take heart and be strong, knowing He has great things in store for you! Place your hope in Jesus, Whose love never fails!

SEPTEMBER 9TH RUNNING WITH PET PEEVES

"Do to others as you would have them do to you." (Luke 6:31 NIV)

Cars that pass too close and lawn mowers that cut grass beside you are just two of many pet peeves that runners might have. Annoyances happen not only in running but in everyday life! Leaving dirty socks on the floor, cracking knuckles, and driving under the speed limit could fall on any number of lists! We all have pet peeves that drive us batty each and every day.

So although we do not have control of other's actions, we do have control of the attitude to which we respond. Instead of letting others crawl under our skin and turn our reaction into something ugly, we can treat others with mercy and grace. We are all called to live lives that emulate Christ's love inside us! We are living examples of God who lives inside of us. You never know how your words or actions done in Christ's name might be a seed of faith, which is planted in the heart of someone else. Show others the love you want to see in return!

SEPTEMBER 10ᵀᴴ SENT FEET

And how can anyone preach unless they are sent? As it is written, "How beautiful are the feet of those who bring good news!" (Romans 10:15 NIV)

Where do you run? If you are fortunate you have an amazing place to roam at your pleasure. All you have to do is step out your door and a beautifully safe place sprawls before your feet. However, most runners have to get to the place where they are going to start their run. Some runners are restricted by their climate, other runners by their schedule, and still others by their location. Whatever the reason, most runners have to go to where the workout is!

Telling others about Jesus is a lot like finding the right place to start your workout. How can you reach others for Jesus if you are sitting on the couch staring at your television? Unfortunately, it just doesn't work that way! We have to go to where the people are! Where is God calling you to go? Maybe God is calling you to go and share the good news of salvation with your neighbors, friends, classmates, family, or a total stranger who lives halfway across the globe. So what are you waiting for? Go and get busy!

SEPTEMBER 11ᵀᴴ TRADING SLIPPERS FOR SNEAKERS

God made him who had no sin to be sin for us, so that in him we might become the righteousness of God. (2 Corinthians 5:21 NIV)

Unbeknownst to you, you made a trade. Yes you did! When you became a runner you made the unconscious decision to swap in your comfy house slippers for a pair of running shoes. You said no to a life of lying around the house and said yes to a new and beautiful adventure that promises to challenge you each and every day!

Someone else also made a trade, but this time in your place! Jesus took the death we deserved. Jesus took our place on the cross. This means that there is nothing we can do or will ever do to earn salvation. Nothing! Jesus paid it all! All we have to do is believe!

"They replied, "Believe in the Lord Jesus, and you will be saved-you and your household."" (Acts 16:31 NIV)

SEPTEMBER 12ᵀᴴ THE RUN AGAINST TIME

Teach us to number our days, that we may gain a heart of wisdom. (Psalm 90:12 NIV)

No time for a run? Uh oh! The race against time is a losing one! Somewhere sandwiched between your job, spouse, kids, homework, shopping, dinner, holidays, volunteering, laundry, dishes, mowing the lawn, friends, running errands, vacuuming, dusting, and cleaning the car you have to fit in your run! As difficult as it is to squeeze in a workout, it proves even more difficult to spend time with God.

We are busy and rightly so, but never discredit every precious moment spent with our Father! God wants to be close to you! So hide your smart phone, shut the door, and leave the worries of the world behind as you dive between the pages of God's Word!

SEPTEMBER 13ᵀᴴ RUNNING WITH PERSEVERANCE

"But he knows the way that I take; when he has tested me, I will come forth as gold." (Job 23:10 NIV)

Every run is a test of endurance. No matter what the length! As a runner we are often pushed to the brink, giving it our all. Runners are required to dig from way down deep and pull themselves together to give it their all, even when there isn't much left to give. Like running, our life is full of tests and trials that leave us shaky and uncertain if we will be able to make it.

Are you going through a season of life that is testing your strength, your endurance? Feel as if you are at your wit's end, unable to muster the strength to take one step more? God loves you. God loves you so much more than you could ever fathom or even imagine! As our Father, He calls His children to live lives that glorify Him in heaven. Living life as a child of God is tough work! We have pretty tough shoes to fill: to walk as Jesus did! But no matter what you are facing or what you may be going through, God is always there, always beside you every step of the way. Your Father will always give you the strength to do His will.

SEPTEMBER 14ᵀᴴ RUNNING TRADITIONS

"But as for me and my household, we will serve the LORD." (Joshua 24:15b NIV)

Does running "run" in your family? Living within a family of other runners is a wonderful way to feel the camaraderie and support that can only come from those who understand! They understand the aches, the sweat, and the tears that running brings!

Just the same, being a part of a family of believers makes living for Christ so much easier! Rejoice with gladness that your family has life everlasting! But if not, that's okay too. That just means it's time to get busy! You now have the important job of sharing, giving, and showing Jesus love to them. Every member in your family is so important to God! God loves and cares for them and is calling you to reach them with the gospel! So faithfully tell them, diligently share God's love with them, and continually pray for them! Be a prayer warrior for your family. Be bold, be brave, and share the love of Christ with your family!

SEPTEMBER 15TH RUNNER'S DOUBT

But when you ask, you must believe and not doubt, because the one who doubts is like a wave of the sea, blown and tossed by the wind. (James 1:6 NIV)

You are in the middle of a race. The big event you have been faithfully and diligently training months for. Your breath is coming hard and fast. Sweat is pouring down your face. You are pushing yourself as hard and as fast as your muscular legs can possibly go. You literally feel like you are going to break. Doubt starts to creep in. Urges to slow to a walk begin to swirl inside your mind. Crossing the finish line is starting to feel impossible. Unreachable!

Doubt is just one of the emotions we as runners deal with again and again. Even with proper training, doubt rears its ugly head. Always remember, doubt has no power over you! We never have to distrust the strength we have in Christ! We never have to doubt God's love for us. We never have to question God's forgiveness, goodness, or mercy! They are new and overflowing every day.

Run and live confidently within God's grace and mercy every day!

SEPTEMBER 16TH RUN JUST AS YOU ARE

And we know that in all things God works for the good of those who love him, who have been called according to his purpose. (Romans 8:28 NIV)

We all yearn to be quick and nimble footed. Effortlessly gliding! Truth is none of us run the exact same way! Some of us are quirky in every movement we take. Some of us are slow but steady, while others are as quick as lightning. Thank You God that we all run differently! Thank God that He has blessed each and every one of us to look and act independently.

We are to run just as we are and we are to live just as God made us to live! We all have unique shoes to fill in God's kingdom! So be the person God created you to be! Use the gifts God has given you to glorify Him! Make good use of the talents He has blessed you with. The rest of the world is waiting for you to use your unique gifts to serve your King!

SEPTEMBER 17TH RUNNING TENTATIVELY

Be kind and compassionate to one another, forgiving each other, just as in Christ God forgave you. (Ephesians 4:32 NIV)

Too scared to run again? Starting to run again can be scary, even after getting the okay from your doctor after a serious or even mild injury. Thoughts of re-injury hauntingly swirl inside your head as you take your first steps especially when fears of being laid up on the couch again wildly heckle your peace. So maybe you have never suffered from a running injury but maybe you have experienced hurt by another person.

We are all human; we are all vulnerable to injured feelings and the possibility of doing the same to others. However, just because you were hurt by someone else, does not mean that you cannot learn to move on, to heal, and to forgive. Forgiving can be scary, even painful, but it is impossible to move forward, without the courage and strength that comes from Jesus.

If you have a past hurt that you are unable to overcome, give it to Jesus! God can heal a broken and bruised heart, show you how to forgive, and teach you how to run forward!

SEPTEMBER 18TH RUN ON!

Brothers and sisters, I do not consider myself yet to have taken hold of it. But one thing I do: Forgetting what is behind and straining toward what is ahead, (Philippians 3:13 NIV)

You blew it! You do not know how but you failed! Big time! You trained faithfully, built super high hopes, and when the big race came… you fell short.

In life we have plenty of ups and downs. Things happen, bad things. We experience money problems, job loss, family and friend feuds, and personal loss. We all fall short. We all have struggles. All of us! However, it is not what we have done but what we do once when we get back up. Do we whine, complain, and dwell in the past or confidently push forward? We have a goal, and that goal and that prize lies in Christ Jesus! We are to live a life that brings glory and honor to God. Leave the past in the dust then press forward to who God is calling you to be!

SEPTEMBER 19TH RUN BY FAITH

For we live by faith, not by sight. (2 Corinthians 5:7 NIV)

It's completely pitch black outside. You cannot see a thing, not even your hand! You are running as blind as a bat. You faintly hear something in the distance. It sounds as though someone is calling you by your name. You attentively focus on the kindhearted voice as you make your way through the darkness. When you carefully concentrate on the voice, your run becomes achievable. But if you stray from the voice you quickly fumble and are easily disoriented and uncertain of which way to go.

As Christians we live by faith not by sight! We must learn to listen to God's voice. We need to follow God's beckoning even when we cannot see. We must learn to turn down the distracting noises of the world that surrounds us and passionately focus on God and on Him alone!

SEPTEMBER 20TH FEET ON THE MOVE

In their hearts humans plan their course, but the LORD establishes their steps. (Proverbs 16:9 NIV)

Left foot, right foot, left foot, right foot, your feet go exactly where you place them! Runners are all too aware of the fact they are in the driver's seat! There is no sitting back and relaxing! Without our driving willpower, pushing and prodding us to go, our feet don't get anywhere!

We are all sitting in the helm in all the decisions we make. God has blessed us with the ability of our own free will. God gave us the freedom to choose to live for and follow Him. God gives us the feet and God gives us the plan for our lives. God calls us to live for Him using the talents and skills He has blessed you with! So just like we have the ability to tell our feet where to go, we must use those hands and feet that God has given us to be on the move for Him!

SEPTEMBER 21ST A RUNNER'S FOUNDATION

So this is what the sovereign LORD says, "See, I lay a stone in Zion, a tested stone, a precious cornerstone for a sure foundation; the one who relies on it will never be stricken with panic." (Isaiah 28:16b NIV)

What's the purpose to which you run? Do you run to fulfill a lifelong goal such as losing weight, raising money for a cause, or to get in shape? We all have an intention when it comes to running otherwise you probably wouldn't do it!

Our lives must mimic the same intention. Jesus must be the cornerstone to which everything else in our lives is built upon. Jesus must be the solid foundation to which we spring forward and be a testimony of His love. When our lives are firmly built on Jesus, no matter what comes against us, we firmly rest in His trustworthy hands! So even when our legs give way, our hearts will never fail when they are firmly rooted in the love of Jesus!

SEPTEMBER 22ND ALMOST THERE!

God is our refuge and strength, an ever-present help in trouble. Therefore we will not fear, though the earth give way and the mountains fall into the heart of the sea, (Psalm 46:1-2 NIV)

You can see it off in the distance…the cherished finish line! You are so close you can practically feel it! But you still have quite a ways to go! The gap that separates you from the freedom of walking feels so long, so far! However you keep going, you keep trucking along with every ounce of free energy left.

Life can often feel that way. You are so close, you can taste it. However, you still have so far to go, so much left to be done. You feel defeated, overwhelmed. You feel as if you just do not have the strength to keep going. But be encouraged! You are never alone! We serve a great God. A God who never leaves, never forsakes. Just ask Him. God will give you the strength! Reach out your hand into God's outstretched grasp and together you can do anything! Nothing absolutely nothing is impossible with God, so keep running, always pressing forward!

SEPTEMBER 23RD HOBBLING AROUND

He heals the brokenhearted and binds up their wounds. (Psalm 147:3 NIV)

What do you do when you start limping? You stop running of course! Most runners would not continue to run!

Are you limping through life? Are you trudging around with an emotional pain that is invisible to the human eye? Are you guarding a pain that is far more paralyzing than any physical pain? Whatever you are going through, whatever agony you might be enduring, you can give your heartache to God!

Just as we were not made to run through pain, we were not made to live with pain! Pain will happen of course but the quicker you give it to the Great Physician the quicker you will begin to heal! Give God your hurts, pains, and heartaches now. You have been emotionally limping around too long!

SEPTEMBER 24TH "I JUST DON'T FEEL LIKE RUNNING!"

Then Jesus said to his disciples, "Whoever wants to be my disciple must deny themselves and take up their cross and follow me." (Matthew 16:24 NIV)

You can make one of two choices; you can either (A) sleep in 45 minutes longer in your warm cozy bed or (B) laboriously thump down a sidewalk in the frigid morning air. Hmm...doesn't seem like that hard of a decision. Good night!

Following Jesus offers much the same choices. We can either (A) follow the world and live to its standards or (B) follow Jesus. Living as the world does is easy, piece of cake! It's when we step out of the world's cookie cutter expectations that things really start to get hard! We don't always feel like following Jesus, instead we want to crawl back to our old ways. However, being a Christian requires following Jesus daily. Every day we must say no to lures of the world and the comforts of ourselves and yes to Christ! Say yes to following Jesus and trusting Him with your time, money, talents, relationships, and even your very life. Following Jesus will not always be comfortable but the joy is undeniable!

SEPTEMBER 25TH RUNNING WITH ASSURANCE

If you declare with your mouth, "Jesus is Lord," and believe in your heart that God raised him from the dead, you will be saved." (Romans 10:9 NIV)

Are your hopes set on a gold medal? Wouldn't it be comforting if you could have the guarantee of winning the trophy even before you set foot on the course? Maybe your sights are not set on a blue ribbon but on just finishing the course. Runners would run so much easier if they just had the promise of completion!

Life, unfortunately, offers very few assurances. But for those who place their faith in Jesus, they live a very different story! Christians have the promise of eternal life that is only offered through faith in Christ! We can live our lives with the joy and peace of knowing that God loves us and we are His! We have eternal life in Christ. Through Jesus, we have the blessed assurance of everlasting life! That is a guarantee that can never be taken away!

SEPTEMBER 26TH CRAZY LEGS!

For I am not ashamed of the gospel, because it is the power of God that brings salvation to everyone who believes: first to the Jew, then to the Gentile. (Romans 1:16 NIV)

Let's face it, running is crazy! It doesn't make any sense that you would want to suffer through any speed that exceeds that of a leisurely walk! Much less undergoing this activity, day after day, week after week, year in and year out! The fact that you find pure joy and pleasure in a venture that most people wouldn't even dream of doing, leaves most non-runners scratching their heads in confusion.

In the same way we must live a life that others would view as "crazy" for our Savior. Following Jesus demands radical devotion and enthusiastic commitment. It requires us to faithfully follow Christ wholeheartedly with everything we are. We are called to unashamedly and unabashedly live for God. Seems kind of backwards from how the world lives, doesn't it? That's because by the world's standard, passionate Christians are kind of kooky! So get out there and live a life that to the world seems crazy for our Savior!

SEPTEMBER 27TH RUN THE RIGHT PATH

You make known to me the path of life; you will fill me with joy in your presence, with eternal pleasures at your right hand. (Psalm 16:11 NIV)

Oh, okay, very nice. I could run on this path all day! It's a wonderfully soft dirt trail, smooth on the feet, and offering delightful scenery to pass the time. Who wouldn't want to take this route? So why do we as Christians so often find ourselves running down the harsh, rocky, brier-lined, poison ivy filled path, all by ourselves!

Maybe you are running down this path in your daily life and don't even know it! Instead of taking the peaceful trail alongside your Heavenly Father; you are all alone, stumbling in the dark and robbed of the joy that comes from following God's will. Maybe it's time to stop, listen to God's voice, and follow His leading. Follow the special path God has called you to in your life!

SEPTEMBER 28TH LOGGING THE MILES

"But blessed is the one who trusts in the LORD, whose confidence is in him. They will be like a tree planted by the water that sends out its roots by the stream. It does not fear when heat comes; its leaves are always green. It has no worries in a year of drought and never fails to bear fruit." (Jeremiah 17:7-8 NIV)

Do you keep a training diary? Diligently writing down a daily journal to track your running story, your progress, and your hardships? As you look through its pages it is easy to see your progress and how far you have already come!

Okay, so now that you are keeping tabs of your progress are you keeping track of all that God has done in your life this year? That's right. It's time to write down and record your growth, your prayers, and all the areas you have to give thanks to

God! A great way to recall God's blessings and answered prayers is to write them in a diary of gratitude! You will be utterly blown away with amazement with all the blessings God has rained down on your life throughout the year. Our God is good! Amen!

SEPTEMBER 29TH RUNNING ON THE EDGE

"As for us, we cannot help speaking about what we have seen and heard." (Acts 4:20 NIV)

Imagine you are sprinting as hard as you can straight up a mountain trail. The only thing in front of you is a rough, rocky trail. Your heavy breath is coming hard and fast. You are tired, exhausted, and ready to call it quits! Every step you take is apprehensive and you are unsure if you can even make it! To become a better, faster runner we often have to push past our comfort zones, don't we?

You know what else pushes us out of our comfort zone? Sharing the gospel! We can feel overwhelmed, scared, and uncomfortable! We are unconfident if we can even do this! But hold on. You can do it! With the love and strength of The One living inside you, you can loudly proclaim His story and His love. God loves you so much that He sent His one and only Son to die in your place! Now that kind of love is worth sharing!

SEPTEMBER 30TH TAKE THEM UP ON THAT RUN!

"Do you understand what you are reading?" Peter asked. "How can I," he said, "unless someone explains it to me?" (Acts 8:30b-31a NIV)

"I wish I could run like you!" Sound like familiar words? Faithfully committed runners hear this from their non-running friends all the time. But how often do you do something about it. Next time you hear this comment, lovingly step in alongside them and encourage them in their dream to run. Take the time to answer questions and give advice when needed.

How often in our faith walk do we witness the same phenomena with others coming alongside us asking about our faith in Jesus Christ? How often do they show interest in the reason for our joy and yet we fail to take their hand and run with them on a journey of living for Christ? So make a point to take someone up on that challenge, not only physically race beside them, but come alongside encouraging them on the most important run of all, living for Jesus!

OCTOBER 1ST RUN BECAUSE YOU ARE WORTH IT!

Do you not know that your bodies are temples of the Holy Spirit, who is in you, whom you have received from God? You are not your own; you were bought at a price. Therefore honor God with your bodies. (1 Corinthians 6:19-20 NIV)

Whew! You plop down on the kitchen chair exhausted. You would really love to go out on a run but as you gaze over the kitchen, you realize that your workout is at the bottom of an unending to-do list. Our busy lifestyles and our overstocked schedules leave very little time for taking care of ourselves. Between transporting kids to and from school and making sure everyone is fed and clothed, exercising falls to the bottom of the barrel. But you forgot one very important thing. You are worth it!

You are worth the time spent keeping your body healthy! You are so valuable! God loves you so much that He sent His only Son into this world to die a horrible death on the cross that through life in Jesus Christ, we may live forever. Now that's true love isn't it? Our bodies are the temple of God and knowing that, we must treat our bodies with the respect they deserve. So honor God with your body! You are worth it!

OCTOBER 2ND A RUNNER'S MASSAGE

For sin shall no longer be your master, because you are not under the law, but under grace. (Romans 6:14 NIV)

Yep that's the spot! As a runner, who doesn't love a pampering massage? Massages are one of a runner's best friends for rubbing out muscle soreness and those nagging pressure points. Just like a runner rubs out those aches and pains, we as Christians need to be working on the trouble spots in our hearts. As a runner we proactively work out those tight areas so that we can be faster, better runners.

As Christians, we need to be actively seeking those "sin spots" that slow us down in our walk with Christ. So what areas are deterring you from a closer relationship with God? Is there an area in your life that is slowing you down or holding up your growth in Christ?

OCTOBER 3RD THE DETAILS OF RUNNING

These have come so that the proven genuineness of your faith-of greater worth than gold, which perishes even though refined by fire- may result in praise, glory and honor when Jesus Christ is revealed. (1 Peter 1:7 NIV)

"Wait! I didn't sign up for this!"

Do you sometimes feel as if you did not sign up for all the intricate details of running? You feel as if you failed to read all of the fine print when you first began. You want to get fit; you just don't want to, well, run all those miles! A Christian might exclaim much the same,

"I didn't sign up for this either!"

As the Holy Spirit works in our hearts and minds He wields us, molds us, and works us to become more and more like Jesus. It can be hard, tough, difficult, and you might have to give up things and habits that are familiar and comfortable. However the prize we run towards is worth all the pain! The life giving joy we discover in Christ is always worth whatever we give up, whatever we suffer through, and whatever we come against!

OCTOBER 4TH RUNNING SCARED

"For I am the LORD your God who takes hold of your right hand and says to you, Do not fear; I will help you." (Isaiah 41:13 NIV)

You take a step and then timidly glance behind your left shoulder. You take another step then nervously look behind you. You step again, checking your shadow this time instead. Maybe you have never ran with the hyper vigilance of an inquisitive cat but perhaps you are going through life as if something bad is lurking behind every mysterious corner.

Perhaps you do not fear the known but the unknown. Maybe you hide in fear of the endless possibilities that could happen. You fear the problem's of the future. The anxiety of the unknown might be robbing you of living your life to the fullest today. Is fear stripping you of your joy and your peace? The great news is you do not have to be afraid, God is right beside you! You and everything else in your future is in God's hands! In your Father's perfect, capable hands! It is important that you trust Him, with not only your today, but your tomorrow!

OCTOBER 5TH RUN AND PRAY

Therefore confess your sins to each other and pray for each other so that you may be healed. The prayer of a righteous man is powerful and effective. (James 5:16 NIV)

You are in the middle of a relaxing run. It's a beautiful sunny day with a light, playful breeze that gently fans your face. You have nothing ahead of you but freedom and an open pathway. So what do you do? You pray! Use today's run time to lift up others in prayer. Pray for your family; ask that they would know Jesus as their Lord and Savior. Pray for your co-workers, neighbors, friends, and others you encounter every day. Pray that they would see Jesus living inside of you.

Pray for our brothers and sisters in Christ who are being persecuted, attacked, and standing trial because of their faith in Jesus Christ. Pray that God would give them the strength and courage to stand firm in their faith, and that they would find true joy in Jesus. Pray for those who do not know Jesus. Pray for those who adamantly refuse to believe or laugh at you for your faith. Pray that God would open their hearts and their minds to His Word. Run to Pray!

OCTOBER 6TH RUN AS YOU ARE

But God demonstrates his own love for us in this: While we were still sinners, Christ died for us. (Romans 5:8 NIV)

Runners come in all varieties; short, tall, small, large, athletic, and just starting out! Athletes toe the starting line in all shapes, sizes, and abilities! Contrary to popular belief, you do not have to be super fit to start running! You do not have to be in the best shape of your life, you can just start from where you are today!

Sometimes people do not think they can follow Jesus until they become a better person. They convince themselves that they are just not "good enough" and that they have done too much wrong to be forgiven. News flash! Christians are far from perfect! Quite the opposite! The only difference between a believer and a non-believer is a believer knows they are saved by the perfect blood of Jesus Christ. Christians are far from perfect; they just follow a perfect Savior. As Christians we don't suddenly arrive sinless, but instead become increasingly like Christ. It is a daily journey, a daily struggle. So if you are unsure about Jesus and do not think you can come to Him as you are, think again! God wants you now. Just as you are!

OCTOBER 7TH TREADMILL OF THOUGHTS

We demolish arguments and every pretension that sets itself up against the knowledge of God, and we take captive every thought to make it obedient to Christ. (2 Corinthians 10:5 NIV)

Around and around, around and around it goes! The smooth belt of the treadmill is continually revolving! You get a workout in but you actually get nowhere! Like the rotation of the treadmill is the one track, anxious mind. We turn the same negative thoughts over and over inside our mind dwelling on what cannot be changed by worry and what might not ever happen. Jesus said, "Can any one of you by worrying add a single hour to your life?" (Matthew 6:27 NIV)

Instead of focusing on the ugly and the bad, maybe it's time to turn those worrying thoughts over to God and focus on Him! Anxieties and fears are opportunities to trust God! Turn your worry into praise!

OCTOBER 8TH RUNNING THROUGH HEARTACHE

"Do not let your hearts be troubled. You believe in God; believe also in me." (John 14:1 NIV)

Loss is hard. Loss can feel consuming, making it impossible to do anything else, much less run. Loss can arrive in any number of hosts, such as a death of a loved one, unemployment, loss of a dream, loss of possessions, or divorce. During these times we feel crippled, lost in the dark, fumbling for a new direction. You feel as though you are running through life alone, as if no one else understands the pain you're going through.

God is there and He is just waiting for you to come to Him with all the brokenness and the helplessness you are experiencing. So often during these times of heartache we tend to run away from God and chose to run a route all by ourselves, isolated and afraid. However, it is within these tear-filled moments that when we turn from ourselves and seek our Maker, that true healing can begin. Run to the comfort of God's welcoming arms.

October 9th Impromptu Runner

Be wise in the way you act toward outsiders; make the most of every opportunity. (Colossians 4:5 (NIV)

Okay, you have thirty minutes… That window of opportunity, no matter what the length of time, you immediately snatch it up and go on a run! Just as any moment is an opportunity to run; as a child of God we should take advantage of every chance that is presented to share the good news of salvation!

No matter where you are or what you are doing, we should gladly share Christ's love with anyone in earshot. The possibilities are endless! You can tell the person sitting beside you on the bus, your fellow coworker sitting across from you at lunch, or the neighbor living across the street. Christ's love has no boundaries and neither should we! Ask God to give opportunities and open doors to share His love to hearts that are open and ready! Make use of each and every opportunity you "run into"!

OCTOBER 10TH LAUNCHING OFF THE COUCH

"The gatekeeper opens the gate for him, and the sheep listen to his voice. He calls his own sheep by name and leads them out." (John 10:3 NIV)

Unfortunatly we are unable to run from the comfort of our living room sofa! If we could we would all probably have the physique of an Olympic athlete. In running, participation is required. Just like your call to leave the comfort of your couch to run the race of a healthier you, is the call of God in our lives.

God calls our name from wherever we are and in whatever we are doing; to live a life that is pleasing to our Heavenly Father. So what are you waiting for? Kick those feet into gear and live the life for Christ you were called to live! What will you do with your calling?

October 11th Running In Between

Very early in the morning, while it was still dark, Jesus got up, left the house and went off to a solitary place, where he prayed. (Mark 1:35 NIV)

Life hosts a lot of in-betweens, doesn't it? There are many things, projects, and people that get between us and what we want we really want to be doing like running! Overtime at work, school projects, obligations, and just being flat out tired can separate you from the open road, track, or trail. Running is one thing but what happens when we let life get between us and God! Uh oh! Now it's time to pay attention!

So often we fill our lives with more and more "stuff"! These extracurricular activities might even be godly activities like volunteering at church or serving at a soup kitchen. Even so, it's important not to let the relationships we have with other things and people, interfere with the most important relationship we will ever have; the relationship between you and God.

So take time today to de-clutter the extra "stuff" in your life and pave the way for more time with God!

OCTOBER 12TH IF IT ISN'T "THIS" IT'S "THAT"

I sought the LORD, and he answered me;

he delivered me from all my fears. (Psalm 34:4 NIV)

You hobble your way into bed. You ache everywhere! If it's not your calf muscles it's your ankles. If it's not your knees it's your quads. If it's not your quads it's your hamstrings! Running really brings out the aches!

Life is full of aches! If it's not "this" it's "that"! Being a Christian does not exempt us from troubles or hardships. As Christians we will face them all day long! However it's not the troubles that we face that are unique; it is who we face them with. Jesus! We can lean on God! Give God your troubles all day long! It can kind of be like the belt on the treadmill that continually circles around and around. As the world sends us trouble; we immediately give them over to God. Get one problem, give it to God. Get another one, give it to God. Give your "this" and your "that's" to God! We were not made to run with them alone!

OCTOBER 13ᵀᴴ RUNNING IS RUNNING

Jesus Christ is the same yesterday and today and forever. (Hebrews 13:8 NIV)

What do dashing through the woods, racing around the track, darting down the street, scurrying down the sidewalk, pattering through the rain, scampering under the sun, pouncing through the snow, and sprinting on the treadmill all have in common? You are running! No matter where you or what you are running through, you are always a runner! No matter what!

Guess what else doesn't change? God! God is always the same, unchanging! That means God's love never ends. Our Father's forgiveness is always extended. God's peace is always waiting. God's grace is always given. So even though we live in a world that is always moving, always changing, we serve a God who remains unvarying. Run in Christ's everlasting love, grace, and mercy today!

OCTOBER 14ᵀᴴ TAKING THE EASY ROAD

"My feet have closely followed his steps; I have kept to this way without turning aside." (Job 23:11 NIV)

You have a decision to make. You can either run the route to your left, a strenuous path that transports you straight up a long mountain climb. Or you can choose the path to your right, an easy serene path through the tranquil woods. Seems like a pretty effortless pick!

Life continually presents us with easier routes. As Christians we are surrounded by them. It would be so much simpler to just go with the crowd and do what everyone else is doing! It would be so much easier to say what everyone else says and live as the world expects! But that isn't you or who God created you to be! No, you stand up against the grain! Yes the right road is uphill, bumpy, and sweaty but it is the road God is leading you to take. So run on! Not only is God leading you but He is right beside you!

OCTOBER 15TH REGULAR CHECKUPS REQUIRED

Above all else, guard your heart, for everything you do flows from it. (Proverbs 4:23 NIV)

Stick out your tongue and say "AHHH!" Going to the doctor regularly is super important. Getting the green light from your doctor before starting any exercise plan is the best place to start! As vital as it is to keep a pulse on your physical health it is just as important as it to guard your heart spiritually!

What's the condition of your spiritual heart look like? Is your heart soft and moldable in your Father's hands or does anger, malice, guilt, and un-forgiveness rot inside? Are you holding on to something that went bad or a hurt someone else caused you? Maybe you are holding unto a pain that is so deep and hurtful that it is preventing you from living a joyful, happy, and fulfilling life. Give God your pain. Give God your sadness. Give God your hurt. Ask God today to help you have a heart that can be used by Him!

OCTOBER 16TH RUNNING TRANSFORMATION

Do not conform to the pattern of this world, but be transformed by the renewing of your mind. Then you will be able to test and approve what God's will is-his good, pleasing and perfect will. (Romans 12:2 NIV)

Running creates a body transformation! Runners must condition their bodies and minds to run the race and complete the task that lies ahead of them!

In the same way, when we accept Jesus as our Lord and Savior, we undergo a transformation too, from the inside! We now get to live our lives for Christ, a life that points others to God and brings glory to His name!

We must live our lives in a way that says no to the lures of the world and says yes to the things that please our Heavenly Father. This can be tough. The world tries to pull us away from God in many different ways! But hold fast and stay true!

"You, dear children, are from God and have overcome them, because the one who is in you is greater than the one who is in the world." (1 John 4:4 NIV) Always remember you are an over comer!

OCTOBER 17TH PRESS ON!

I press on toward the goal to win the prize for which God has called me heavenward in Christ Jesus. (Philippians 3:14 NIV)

As runners we can easily understand and embrace this message! Runners "press on" and "strain toward" the reward that lies behind that prized finish line ahead of us. We are focused and intentional about our training in order to complete our race to the best of our ability. Just as we strive and train as runners, we must also strive to grow in Christ.

Our salvation is not something we need to earn or work for because it is given freely through faith in Christ! As we continue to mature, we seek to become more and more like Christ. We are called to live lives that glorify God. We are called for a glorious purpose!

OCTOBER 18ᵀᴴ RUNNING WITH GRATITUDE

Give thanks to the LORD, for he is good; his love endures forever. (1Chronicles 16:34 NIV)

God is good, pure and holy! But do you ever take the time to consider and ponder the goodness of God in your heart? Our God is gracious and He is so good to us. Our Father abundantly showers grace, mercy, and love on the earth. None of these gifts, have we ever deserved! Every step you take is because of God's greatness, grace, and love.

What does the goodness of God look like in your life? Have you thanked God for all He has done, is doing, and will do in your life? Take time on your run today to thank God for His kindness. Bask in God's grace. Consider your King's mercies within your heart and ask Him how to show His goodness through you unto others.

OCTOBER 19ᵀᴴ THE MEAT AND POTATOES OF RUNNING

"Therefore everyone who hears these words of mine and puts them into practice is like a wise man who built his house on the rock." (Matthew 7:24 NIV)

Proper shoes are the firm foundation to which any runner stands on, literally! A great pair of shoes is the base to which all the miles are built upon. Like building your training upon the proper footwear is like the wise builder who built his house upon the rock.

As Christians we are called to put into practice the words of God! We are called to put God's words into actions! So just like putting those flashy new shoes to the pavemen,t go and do what God calls us to do! Even though the rains may fall, the streams may rise, and the winds blow against you, the solid foundation you have in Jesus Christ will never fall!

OCTOBER 20TH RUNNING RIGHT BY

If anyone, then, knows the good they ought to do and doesn't do it, it is sin for them. (James 4:17 NIV)

It's a beautiful morning as you energetically sprint around your neighborhood block. You turn the corner and as you always do and spot your neighbor struggling to get her bulky trash to the curb. Instead of stopping and assisting your neighbor, the wheels in your head start to turn. You begin to reason; she will be able to do it, right? Sure, she always does, every Wednesday. You, on the other hand, have limited time before you have to be at work, and this is the only time you have today to run. So… you run right past.

This has never happened to you, right? Of course it has! Seeing someone in need and not helping them happens. To everyone! So today is the day to stop strolling by and start taking the time to do what is right! What is it that God is showing you to do? Be the love of Jesus you wish to see!

OCTOBER 21ST HERE'S YOUR RUNNING INVITE

Remember this: Whoever turns a sinner from the error of their way will save them from death and cover over a multitude of sins. (James 5:20 NIV)

Who inspired you?! Was it your neighbor, friend, sister, brother, or co-worker? Did you see them running and want to be like them, look like them, and run just like them. Congratulations you did just that, you started running!

To be saved by the blood of Jesus, you have to make a decision. You have to accept Jesus as your Lord and Savior, turning away from your old sin and starting a new life in Him, but someone had to share with you the need for this decision! Someone had to listen to the call of God in their lives to share the good news with you! Who was it that told you, encouraged you, or pointed you to Christ? Was it something they said, the joy they held, or the way they acted that drew you to them? Whoever that wonderful person was, thank them for their faithfulness to do what God has commanded us all to do, make disciples! So in turn, who can you tell, invite, or encourage? Who is God calling you to deliver that life saving invite to?

OCTOBER 22ND RUNNING LEGACY

A good name is more desirable than great riches; to be esteemed is better than silver or gold. (Proverbs 22:1 NIV)

What legacy will you leave? Will people commemorate you for a running record you triumphantly broke, or will they remember the marathons you proudly finished, or will they recall the countless miles you faithfully added up day after day after day? When you run, run with all your heart and when you live, live in a way that points to Jesus.

Live your life in a way that others would see Jesus living in you. Live life in a way so that you represent Christ in everything you do! Living a life dedicated to running is a great way to be remembered but living a life faithfully committed to Jesus is timeless! How many people will be in heaven because God used you to lead them to Jesus? Leave a legacy! A legacy that points others to Christ!

OCTOBER 23ᴿᴰ MESSY STARTS

The name of the LORD is a fortified tower; the righteous run to it and are safe. (Proverbs 18:10 NIV)

It's a disaster! You literally feel like a scarf unraveling at both ends. When life gets messy and it always does, it can be difficult to leave things undone and just head out for your daily run. But it is so important to remember that although the predicament you are facing will still be there when you get back; you will come back from your run feeling better equipped to handle the challenge. Taking a second to walk away and meet with God in the middle of your troubles is the best thing you can do.

However, it is usually during these chaotic times that we hide from God; maybe we even blame Him for the mess. Our journey is marked by constant trials and growing pains, it has to be in order to become increasingly like Christ! So stop what you are doing and give God your clutter, your muddle, your shambles, and your chaos. Run to God and the safety of His presence; surrender whatever it is you are going through to Him today.

OCTOBER 24ᵀᴴ RUNNING DOWN SLEEP

On my bed I remember you; I think of you through the watches of the night. Because you are my help, I sing in the shadow of your wings. I cling to you; your right hand upholds me. (Psalm 63:6-8 NIV)

Missing those ZZZs? Not getting enough sleep? When you run hard you need to match all that hard work with adequate sleep! It is so important to recharge those batteries in order to get up and back on your feet for your next run! Without much sleep, running can be so much harder than it has to be!

Life is chock-full of deadlines, difficulties, and to-do lists with a good night's sleep falling somewhere near the bottom of the barrel. We often go through life half awake, exhausted, tired, and snappy. We deny our bodies the required sleep we desperately need. God offers a rest that is even more important than sleep, a rest that our souls and hearts are yearning for! A peaceful rest from our burdens, struggles, and challenges. Find rest in the peace and protection of God's loving arms!

OCTOBER 25ᵀᴴ IT'S YOUR DECISION

Peter replied, "Repent and be baptized, every one of you, in the name of Jesus Christ for the forgiveness of your sins. And you will receive the gift of the Holy Spirit." (Acts 2:38 NIV)

Okay, times up! Is today the day you start running? Today is the day you can say good- bye to the excuses and yes to working out! You can do it! You can run. You can exercise, eat healthy, and be a healthier version of who God created you to be! Put some will behind that power and run out the door with some serious will-power! You have already made one life changing decision, but the most important question still remains.

Who is Jesus to you? Was Jesus just a miracle worker? Was Jesus just a proph-et? Is Jesus just a name you say? Is Jesus just someone you sing songs about every Christmas? Or is Jesus your Lord and Savior! Is Jesus the reason you have the promise of everlasting life? Is Jesus your hope and your salvation? Will you choose to trust in Jesus? Will you choose to put your faith in Him today? What decision will you make?

OCTOBER 26ᵀᴴ THE ULTIMATE RUNNER

But Jonah ran away from the LORD and headed for Tarshish. He went down to Joppa, where he found a ship bound for that port. After paying the fare, he went abroad and sailed for Tarshish to flee from the LORD. (Jonah 1:3 NIV)

Jonah was the ultimate runner in the Bible! Wasn't he? God gave Jonah a job to do: to go to Nineveh and preach repentance and what did Jonah do instead? He ran! Jonah ran from the Lord and from the calling God had told Him to do. So often as Christians we find ourselves running away from God don't we?

Running from what we know God has called and commanded us to do. We think we know what is best for our lives! What is God calling you to do? Do you feel the Holy Spirit nudging you to do something important for His Kingdom?

Don't run away, run to God and the task He has called you to do! Run with your calling, not from it!

OCTOBER 27ᵀᴴ RUNNING A GOOD RACE

I have fought the good fight, I have finished the race, I have kept the faith. Now there is in store for me the crown of righteousness, which the Lord, the righteous Judge, will award to me on that day- and not only to me, but also to all who have longed for his appearing. (2 Timothy 4:7-8 NIV)

Runners give it their all! They train hard, eat healthy, and finish strong. Runners discipline their bodies to not only complete the required mileage but to earn the medal they have so faithfully trained for.

As Christians we are also running a race. We run a race that at the finish line, awaits the victor's crown of salvation. This prize is awarded to us through faith in Christ Jesus. Until that day, we run hard and give our best. We strive not because our trophy depends on it, but because we desire to run a race that brings glory and honor to our Heavenly Father. Because of God's great love for us, we in turn push on and finish strong!

OCTOBER 28ᵀᴴ UNTRAINED RUNNER

For our struggle is not against flesh and blood, but against the rulers, against the authorities, against the powers of this dark world and against the spiritual forces of evil in the heavenly realms. (Ephesians 6:12 NIV)

Uh oh! You have a race next week and you have not put in any training, not even a mile! Racing without putting in the proper training can lead to pretty poor results. You might be able to pull off a quick 5k but you probably wouldn't get away with a race such as a marathon without putting the appropriate time in the bank. Without the proper training, we are unable not only physically, but to mentally meet the demands of the race.

In the same way we need to be prepared to stand and fight. Our struggle is not against flesh and blood, but against evil! Satan is on the prowl! (1 Peter 5:8) It's time to strengthen our hands and feet; and prepare our hearts and minds to stand against him! God has given us the tools and the weapons to stand and fight! (Ephesians 6:10-18) Get ready, it is time to go to work! Put on the armor of God and let's get busy!

OCTOBER 29TH NEVER GIVE UP!

Now faith is confidence in what we hope for and assurance about what we do not see. (Hebrews 11:1 NIV)

You are so close! You are almost there! Don't give up, you can finish! When we are just footsteps away from achieving our goal, the way can suddenly seem impossible.

Life can feel the exact same way. Just moments before reaching our ambitions we can become discouraged and lose faith in our ability. We hear ourselves and others convincing us that we are not good enough, strong enough, and capable enough! But as runners and most especially as Christians that is not the way we are called to live! Faith is not always seeing but believing! Believing that God is for us and that He loves us! Faith trusts that no matter what happens or what may come your way, you are in God's loving hands. Never give up, even when the going gets tough! You can and will achieve when you believe!

"For the Spirit God gave us does not make us timid, but gives us power, love and self-discipline." (2 Timothy 1:7 NIV)

OCTOBER 30TH THIS RUN IS RIDICULOUS!

The righteous cry out, and the LORD hears them; he delivers them from all their troubles. (Psalm 34:17 NIV)

Sweat pours down your face like hot water falling from a faucet. Somewhere, along your run you must have missed the correct trail marker. So not only are you miserable but you are lost! You just want to quit! Every step you take seems impossible. But wait, what is that in the distance? You immediately recognize the trail. As your surroundings become familiar, you realize you are not too far from where you initially started. An intense sense of joy washes over you. You can make it, you have been here before!

Sound familiar? Maybe this is how you feel in your life right now. Over-whelmed, lost, and feeling as if you cannot take one more step! The taxing situation you are currently facing is more than you can handle! But you have been here before! You have gone through difficult times like these, and you know what? God has always been there to bring you through! No matter what situation you might be facing, you are not facing them alone! You have nothing to fear! God is always near, always there to get you through!

OCTOBER 31ST ONE GORGEOUS RUN

The heavens declare the glory of God; the skies proclaim the work of his hands. (Psalms 19:1 NIV)

You 'Ooh' and 'aah' as you lovingly gaze upon the breathtaking beauty that surrounds your feet. You cannot help but become awestruck by God's beautiful creation. The trees that were once garnished with the bright green of summer are now elegantly decorated and garnished with buttery yellows, firecracker golds, and cherry reds of the new season. The sun shines, yet not as brightly as summer. Instead a slight coolness has set in to make for an easier and slightly more enjoyable run.

Today remember to run with a deep appreciation of God's magnificent handiwork. Treasure the deep woody smells of the trees, the playfulness of the fall wind, and the wide arrange of color the leaves beautifully wear. Breathe in the goodness of God's creation and have a heart of thankfulness for being able to savor and appreciate the wonders of His hands. Everything on heaven and on earth is the work of God's hands and declares His glory. Take the time to thank your Creator for each and every wonderful thing He has made.

NOVEMBER 1ST MAKING RUNNING A LIFESTYLE

Whom have I in heaven but you?

And earth has nothing I desire besides you. (Psalm 73:25 NIV)

Wow, look at you! You make running look easy! Have you ever noticed that the more you run, the more natural running becomes? You just go do it! Like running, spending time with God, will become easier and easier the more you do it!

The more you delve into God's Word and the more you spend time praying and seeking God, the more it just feels, well natural! Habits are formed by repeatedly doing an activity over and over again. As first it might feel impossible to add one more thing to your schedule. However, the more time you spend in God's presence, the more you desire to seek and to know Him! When you eagerly desire to spend more time in prayer and in God's Word, you will want to leave the hectic ways of the world behind and just lose yourself in your Father's love. Run close to God, each and every day, it's the best habit you will ever form!

NOVEMBER 2ND RUN YOUR MOUNTAIN

No, in all these things we are more than conquerors through him who loved us. (Romans 8:37 NIV)

What goal do you wish to accomplish in running? Do you have visions of throwing your hands up in triumph after finishing a marathon? Or maybe you see yourself sprinting over the finish line of a half marathon. Or perhaps your hopes are set on losing twenty pounds and fitting into that outfit you have been hoping to squeeze into for years.

Maybe the mountain you want to defeat is a life goal. Like owning your own business, witnessing to your neighbor, meeting your future spouse, going on a mission's trip, starting a family, being a part of a church plant, or graduating from college and landing your dream job. Whatever that goal, that achievement, that mountain, it is important to believe in yourself. You can do it! Dream big and believe! Go achieve and strive to do your best! Do whatever God has placed in your heart to do and do it with all your heart for Him and His glory!

NOVEMBER 3ᴿᴰ SERMON RUNNING?

Consequently, faith comes from hearing the message, and the message is heard through the word about Christ. (Romans 10:17 NIV)

Here, put these headphones on! That's right, turn it up! This sermon is in a perfect little audio package and ready to be delivered to your listening ears. Were your children sick, causing you to miss church on Sunday? Better yet, maybe you were at church but want to hear some old sermons from the archives or messages from another church hundreds of miles away!

Tuning in and concentrating on the Word of God while you run, will keep your mind busy and inspired! You will leave your run feeling full of God and ready to go where He leads you! So explore your church's website and discover if they have podcasts or audio sermons available. Watch it as you run on your treadmill or listen to it while you run outside! Strengthen not only your legs, but your hearts and mind!

NOVEMBER 4ᵀᴴ RUNNING AWAY

"Suppose one of you has a hundred sheep and loses one of them. Doesn't he leave the ninety-nine in the open country and go after the lost sheep until he finds it?" (Luke 15:4 NIV)

Uh oh! You strayed from running. Again! You started strong, really strong! You were enthusiastically running almost every day. You were faithfully eating healthy. You had even blown right past your weight loss goal! But then, someway, somehow, you fell right off the wagon of health! Ouch! We all lose interest from time to time, yes even in our running, but have you ever strayed from God?

Just think about it. Maybe at first you were all fired up but then, as time goes on, you have lost that vivaciousness and fire you had for Christ! Do not fret and do not fear, our Heavenly Father is the Good Shepherd and even though we wander off and get distracted, He still loves us! So keep your eyes on Jesus and live with all your might for Him!

NOVEMBER 5TH RUNNING GREEN WITH ENVY

A heart at peace gives life to the body, but envy rots the bones. (Proverbs 14:30 NIV)

You look at their shoes, perfectly fitted for speed. You timidly stare at your own. You examine how they run, as if they were sprinting cheetahs. You self-consciously judge your form. You gaze at their clothes, sleek and expensive. You shyly check out your worn out shorts. Running green with envy does not look good on anyone! Being envious of someone else doesn't look good in any color!

It is so easy to become envious of someone else, especially another Christian! We wish we could sing the way they harmonize or play the guitar the way they strum. We desire to serve God with the gift they were given. We yearn to tell others about Christ with the confidence and boldness they seem to have! But wait! You have something way better! You have your own special talents from God perfectly made for you to use! You are unique! So don't want what they have! Live life the way God made you! Serve, worship, and glorify God using what He has uniquely given you!

NOVEMBER 6TH RUNNING TO TELL THEM

He said to them, "Go into all the world and preach the gospel to all creation." (Mark 16:15 NIV)

You could go on and on and on, and on and on and on about running. Runners can shamelessly and endlessly chatter about their passion for running to anyone and everyone within earshot! No one can hold a candle to your enthusiastic zeal!

However, when it comes to the eternal state of one's soul, we so often don't even bother to approach the topic! It can be difficult at times to tell others about Jesus. Maybe you find it difficult to share your faith or perhaps you are just unsure of how to start. However, through the power and confidence given to us by God, we can openly exclaim the good news to anyone and everyone! The next time you are adamantly sharing about your running, lead into how you are only able to run because of all Jesus has done in your life. Tell them about the hope you have in Jesus and because of that hope you can run freely and passionately. Overflow with the passion you have for Jesus! Let Jesus shine through you and all that you say!

NOVEMBER 7ᵀᴴ RUNNING CLOSE TO JESUS

"I am the vine; you are the branches. If you remain in me and I in you, you will bear much fruit; apart from me you can do nothing." (John 15:5 NIV)

"Jesus, I am stuck on you! I could run in Your love all day long!" Have you experienced the closeness of God when you run? When you actively seek God with an alert mind, a seeking heart, and feet hitting an open road, that's an amazing time to discover His love! As our feet pound the pavement, we feel more vulnerable and more aware of our inability to do things on our own. We are reminded of our total and deep dependence on Him as our Savior.

In the middle of God's breathtaking scenery, we remember just how blessed we are each and every day to enjoy the wonderful activity of running. Stay close to Jesus not only during your workout but within every minute of everyday life. We can do nothing apart from God's deep grace and everlasting love that overflows upon us all.

NOVEMBER 8ᵀᴴ RUN LIKE JESUS

Whoever claims to live in him must walk as Jesus did. (1 John 2:6 NIV)

Take a second and consider. How do you think Jesus would run if He was a runner here on earth today? Would Jesus stop to speak to people as He met them on the road? Would Jesus always halt to assist those that needed help? Would Jesus pause and say hello and smile to everyone He met? Would others feel Christ's love and His presence as He ran?

Would Jesus run with a trailing crowd of mismatched, new, and struggling runners as He lead and encouraged them along? Would people be eager to see Jesus as He ran by? Would strangers flock to the roadside just to get a glimpse of Christ's shadow or touch His clothing as He ran by? We are all called to live like Jesus. To become more and more like Jesus every day! To love as Jesus loved. To forgive as Jesus forgave. To serve as Jesus served. So how can you run more like Jesus today?

NOVEMBER 9TH RUNNING EXCUSES

"Just as the Son of Man did not come to be served, but to serve, and to give his life as a ransom for many." (Matthew 20:28 NIV)

"I'm too tired." "It's too hot out." "It's too cold." "I'm too busy." "Running is too hard." "I just don't like running." I have to clean the house." "I don't have anyone to run with." "I will just run tomorrow." "I just got done eating." "I think I will just sit here instead!"

Running literally creates inventiveness and fabrication in anyone who will do anything to avoid running! The creative juices really start to flow when you try to find a reason not to run! We all have reasons when it comes to skipping our run but what is our excuse for why we don't serve?

The God of the universe came down to earth to serve. So what's our excuse? What is our justification for not helping our neighbor, visiting our friend, or spending time with a lonely family member? What holds us back from sharing the gospel with the person sitting right next to you! Do not fear! Today is a new day! Today is a new opportunity to be the hands and feet of Christ! You can do all things through Christ who gives you strength and courage! You can do it, believe in yourself because God believes in you!

NOVEMBER 10TH SNEAKY RUNNER

"No weapon forged against you will prevail, and you will refute every tongue that accuses you. This is the heritage of the servants of the LORD, and this is their vindication from me," declares the LORD. (Isaiah 54:17 NIV)

You are running all alone. The sleeping city and its inhabitants are still peacefully tucked inside their beds. A crisp morning breeze blows the leaves against the sidewalk as you trudge against it in silence. Then out of nowhere you hear someone, something. You jump! Your skin crawls. Twigs split, rocks crunch, and leaves squeak as another sleepless runner rambles around you and into the morning mist.

Life is like that isn't it? Even when we travel a well-trodden path, we often jump in utter surprise when someone passes our path. Troubles occur much the same way. We expect them to come, yet when they reveal their ugly head, we gasp in complete surprise! Life is full of both surprises and troubles, which are for certain, but no matter what creeps up on you or whatever may leave you breathless, know this: the God who created heaven and earth knows and understands what you are going through. So if the God who created all things is for you, what sneaky, scary thing could ever stand against you?

NOVEMBER 11ᵀᴴ RUNNING WITH HONOR

You, my brothers and sisters, were called to be free. But do not use your freedom to indulge the flesh; rather, serve one another humbly in love. (Galatians 5:13 NIV)

A very special thank you to all you service men and women who have boldly and courageously served in the armed forces! This day is in honor of you! Thank you for all that you have done and all that you continue to do to fight for our freedom! We are so grateful for you!

As Christians, our freedom is found in Jesus. We are granted everlasting life through Jesus who paid it all with His arms lovingly outstretched on the cross. So because of the love God lavishly gives us, let us therefore show love to one another. As you go out on your run today, think of ways you can honor and thank a fellow service man or woman. How can you show them the love of Jesus? Pray for those brave souls who have served or who are currently serving. Lift up their families and loved ones. Show gratitude, give in your special way, love them, and pray for those who fight for your freedom today!

NOVEMBER 12ᵀᴴ RUNNING UNIQUELY

There are different kinds of gifts, but the same Spirit distributes them. There are different kinds of service, but the same Lord. (1 Corinthians 12:4-5 NIV)

Every runner is unique. No two runners are the same! Some runners love running so much that running 26.2 miles is not enough. They have set their sights and feet on ultras! Other runners care less about their distance and focus only on their sheer need for speed! While other runners discover their pleasure not in competition or races but in running itself, they seek to get lost in the quietness of a wooded trail or within the beauty of the hills.

No two runners are the same and neither are any two followers of Christ! We are all different! Unique! We all are given remarkable talents and gifts that are special to how God made us! So rejoice in who God has created you to be! Use the skills God has generously blessed you with to be who He created you to be! Run confidentially in the uniqueness of who God made you to be!

NOVEMBER 13ᵀᴴ THE REASON I RUN

So whether you eat or drink or whatever you do, do it all for the glory of God. (1 Corinthians 10:31 NIV)

Do you run to glorify God or do you run for yourself? Running is a great place to start living for God! When you run, run for God. Glorify God with every step you take, with every thought that you choose to host in your mind, and with every word you say.

As you continually and consciously make an effort to hand over each and every part of your life to God, you will want to do it more and more until there is nothing left. God calls us to live for Him in everything we do. Everything! If you work, work for the Lord. When you drive your car, drive in such a way that brings glory and honor to God. When you love your spouse, your families, and your children love them as Jesus loves. Run to glorify God! It will change not only the way you run but the way you live your life.

NOVEMBER 14ᵀᴴ RUNNING FOR GOOD

Therefore, as we have opportunity, let us do good to all people, especially to those who belong to the family of believers. (Galatians 6:10 NIV)

What cause do you hold close? What breaks your heart or brings a tear to your eye? What do you wish to raise awareness, support, and be a voice for? Is running a platform you can use to show compassion to someone else? Commit today to pray, find, and do something about it! Research causes one to discover where you can show the love of Christ to others around you. Many organizations and charities already hold sponsored events to which you can sign up, join and run!

Once you are signed up, commit to raising awareness and fight for the cause of your heart! As you train, remember to tell others about what you are doing and what the race stands for. Encourage others not only to come and watch but participate themselves. So many people are willing to run or walk for a good cause! Run to spread and share the love of Christ!

NOVEMBER 15ᵀᴴ RUNNER BY DESIGN

The LORD will vindicate me; your love, LORD, endures forever-do not abandon the works of your hands. (Psalm 138:8 NIV)

You are a chosen runner! Specifically chosen to run the race with the gifts and talents God has graciously bestowed on you! You are of special design! Made for a very special purpose! You were lovingly designed by our Creator! God created you with love! Not only did God design you but has a special plan for your life.

That means not only does God know you but He is right beside you every step of the way. Isn't that reassuring? Be a runner after God's own heart. Run in a way that glorifies God. Run in a way that points others to our Savior and King!

NOVEMBER 16TH JUST GIVE ME A CHANCE!

"I love those who love me, and those who seek me find me." (Proverbs 8:17 NIV)

"Just give me a chance, I can do this!" You shout to anyone who disbelieves. You run hard and give your very best each and every time. When others get to know you and get a peek inside your personality, they quickly learn just how driven and passionate you are. You have a heart and feet that are always ready to go!

You know what else is waiting for a chance to show you what's inside? That Bible sitting on your shelf! It is time to crack open the pages and discover who God is. Under the cover, we are introduced to our Creator, our Savior, and King! Inside its pages is where we will meet Jesus, our life, joy, peace, and hope! God's life giving words are yearning to be read! As a runner, you have already proven you are bold and daring, you prove that on your feet! But will you take a chance and start an adventure that lies at the tips of your fingers? If so, it's time to jump in and dive into God's Word today; it's a decision that will leave you coming back for more!

NOVEMBER 17TH RUN WITH GOD

Every good and perfect gift is from above, coming down from the Father of the heavenly lights, who does not change like shifting shadows. (James 1:17 NIV)

Did you take the time to thank God for allowing you to be able to run today? The simple fact that you are able to run should produce gratitude and thankfulness to the Author and Creator of life. Remember to take a moment after every run for the gift of running. Thank God for the time He allowed you to spend with Him, in His presence. Our God is an awesome God! Our King is so worthy of our love and praise. Thank your Creator with every fiber of your being for the ability He has graciously given you.

Heavenly Father, Thank You for this time You have allowed me to spend in Your presence today. Thank You that you have given me the gift and the ability to run. May I always use this gift to bring glory and honor to You. In Jesus name I pray, Amen

NOVEMBER 18TH RESILIENT RUNNER

In fact, everyone who wants to live a godly life in Christ Jesus will be persecuted, (2 Timothy 3:12 NIV)

You are one tough runner! You are a runner, a runner of God! Look at you! You run persistently and triumphantly with the gifts and qualities God has uniquely given you! You are flexible, pliable, and spring back to life every time you are hard pressed! Watch you go!

Everyone who wants to live like Jesus will be persecuted. Everyone! Life is not easy but you will not give up! You are resilient. Chosen and called by Christ to live a life like Christ! You are called to be Christ's hands and feet even when life gets rocky, a little slippery, and incredibly topsy-turvy. In these tough and trying times we have the power of the Holy Spirit living in us! Encouraging us! Pressing us forward!

NOVEMBER 19TH RUNNING UNCERTAIN

"I am God, and there is no other; I am God, and there is none like me. I make known the end from the beginning, from ancient times, what is still to come. I say: 'My purpose will stand, and I will do all that I please.'" (Isaiah 46:9b-10 NIV)

Everything in life is uncertain and that is for certain! As runners we find this particularly true. We can stretch, ice, strengthen, cross train, and faithfully follow a training program and still can become injured! We can train hard and run fast but still not win! We can do everything in our power to run a race and guess what? You can still become sidelined!

It is within our vulnerability we discover God's unlimited capability. We might be weak but God is strong, therefore we can rejoice that we serve a God who has everything in His hands. Our Heavenly Father remains the same today, tomorrow, and forever!

NOVEMBER 20TH ENDURANCE TRAINING

Therefore, since we are surrounded by such a great cloud of witnesses, let us throw off everything that hinders and the sin that so easily entangles. And let us run with perseverance the race marked out for us, (Hebrews 12:1 NIV)

You are proudly strutting down the straightaway to the wild whoops and hollers of your family, friends, and fellow runners. The angst and aches you feel are suddenly thrown off and replaced with strength and courage at the sight of the finish line and the sounds of encouragement,

We all have a race marked out for us! Our Creator and King has a special plan for every one of us! It's time to throw off the heavy sacks of sin that entangles and entraps us and confidently use the talents and skills God has purposed for you! You can do it, through Christ, who gives you peace, power, joy, and strength!

NOVEMBER 21ST STRESS THE SMALL STUFF

"Whoever can be trusted with very little can also be trusted with much, and whoever is dishonest with very little will also be dishonest with much." (Luke 16:10 NIV)

Stress the small stuff? Just hear this out before you judge! Yes it is vital to reap the benefits from all those miles you logged but it can also be just as important to pay attention to the fine, little details. The small stuff! Like what you put into your mouth, the significance of hydration, and adequate rest on those all important recovery days can make all the difference between just watching the race and actually running it!

Are you taking heed to the "small stuff" that could sideline you from a joyous walk with our Savior? Like how you are spending your time? Who you are surrounding yourself with and how they could be influencing you? What are you watching, reading, or listening to? What do the words sound like that come out of your mouth or what do the actions of your hands and feet display? Every little detail makes a difference! Let them make a difference for Jesus!

NOVEMBER 22ND THANKFUL FEET

Rejoice always, (1 Thessalonians 5:16 NIV)

Sniff! Sniff! Smell that? As the aroma of juicy turkey, buttered mashed potatoes, hearty stuffing, mouth watering rolls, and yummy pumpkin pie drift from the kitchen and fill your nostrils, you cannot help but run faster! You woke up extra early to run just in order to fit extra in your belly! Today might be a day dedicated to giving thanks, but we must remember today is not the only time of the year to run thankful!

The Bible tells us to be always joyful! Always, every day of the year, not just the days when there is a turkey happily baking in the oven! So before we roll up our sleeves and dig in, be filled with thanksgiving for our Heavenly Father, our Provider and King! Fill your heart, soul, and mind with thanks for all God has done and continues to do! May every step you take be one of thankfulness, love, and gratefulness to The One who made all things! Make every day a day to give thanks and praise to your Heavenly Father for all He is! Thank you God! Run joyfully always with each and every step you take!

NOVEMBER 23RD OVERTRAINING

"Come to me, all you who are weary and burdened, and I will give you rest. Take my yoke upon you and learn from me, for I am gentle and humble in heart, and you will find rest for your souls. For my yoke is easy and my burden is light." (Matthew 11:28-30 NIV)

Precariously circling the edge of burn out? Are you overtraining in your running? Perhaps you are feeling overtired, sluggish, and quick to become irritable? Maybe you are even losing the smile you once found while running. Burnout does not only occur in running but rears its ugly head in our daily lives!

We can pack our days so full with extra "stuff" that we find ourselves having nothing else to give! Over packing, overextending, and overdoing everything only leaves us feeling exhausted. We come back to God tired, feeling lifeless, with empty hands. However, even though running and giving of our time are great things, it is also important to rest. It is important to seek rest and find console in the presence of our God Almighty. He can give you a peace like none other. Within God's solace we find true peace, love, and joy!

NOVEMBER 24TH RUNNING THROUGH UPS AND DOWNS

Be joyful in hope, patient in affliction, faithful in prayer. (Romans 12:12 NIV)

Up! Down! Up! Down! Running sometimes feels like a twisty roller coaster! Some days are really good, while other workout days feel like you are running with cement in your shoes!

Life often mimics our runs. Some days the sun is shining, birds are chirping, and you feel unstoppable! You feel so close to God. You feel as if your heart could overflow with love and joy for your Savior! While some days feel far from cheery, others feel like a cloud has covered your sunshine. You feel worried and overcome by fear. Down and out and like nothing is going right. Where is God? Does God hear me?

When it feels like your sunshine and joy have disappeared, just remember at these times God is the closest. God desires and longs for you to cast your troubles on Him. God loves you and promises He will never leave us! God is with you through the good, bad, and the ugly!

NOVEMBER 25TH YOU KNOW THIS RUNNER

How, then, can they call on the one they have not believed in? And how can they believe in the one of whom they have not heard? And how can they hear without someone preaching to them? (Romans 10:14 NIV)

Most of the time, it can be pretty easy to spot a fellow runner. Runners are normally either talking about running or out on a run. They come in a wide range of shapes and sizes but one thing always remains, they love to run and they are passionately sharing this love!

In the same way maybe you know those around you who are unbelievers. The important thing is that God has placed that person in your life for a reason. You, yes you, can be the vessel to which the gospel is delivered to a lost and hurting heart. So will you be those shoes that carry the words of everlasting life? Today, is the day to share the news you were born to share!

NOVEMBER 26TH WAKE UP RUNNERS!

"Wake up! Strengthen what remains and is about to die, for I have found your deeds unfinished in the sight of my God." (Revelation 3:2 NIV)

Your breath is coming hard and your feet want to quit. You are close to the finish but still have a bit to go. At times, it can seem that the closer we are to reaching our goal, the further away it is. We are so close to reaching that finish line, yet obstacles and struggles block our victory and overwhelm us with feelings of failure. But do not give up! You're so close, you have come so far, please do not give up now!

It's time for us to wake up Christians! Wake up and move for Jesus! It's time we strap on our shoes and finish the race that we already started. Now is not the time to give up or become dismayed but to feel encouraged and motivated to finish what we already started. God wants to do a great work in you and through you. God wants to use the beautiful gifts He has placed inside of you to glorify Himself. So what are you waiting for, get those feet moving!

November 27th A Runner's Testimony

Many of the Samaritans from that town believed in him because of the woman's testimony, (John 4:39a NIV)

Everyone has a running story, a reason they run! There was a point in your life that you decided to take that first step and move at a pace faster than a walk.

Following Christ also requires a decision. You must resolve to accept Jesus as your personal Lord and Savior. As runners, we have to put in the effort to run if we wish to reap the benefits. As Christians, we are not saved by anything we have done but by what Jesus has already done for us on the cross. Because we are saved and justified by God's grace, we get to live a life that glorifies Him. So run free because Jesus paid it all!

NOVEMBER 28TH NEED A MOMENT?

The Sovereign LORD is my strength; he makes my feet like the feet of a deer, he enables me to tread on the heights. (Habakkuk 3:19 NIV)

Put those feet up! Yep, that's right, find an extra soft spot on a cozy couch to relax your tired body after an extra hard run! Sometimes a moment of rest, especially after a taxing run, is just the ticket to recuperation!

After punching off a long, tiresome shift or after a busy day of caring for your loved ones, you desperately need a moment of peace and quiet. A moment to recollect yourself before you can resume the next project. What's the best way to recharge your low batteries? Spending time with our Lord and Savior! Spending precious time in God's presence is the best action you can take before starting that next item on the to-do list. So open your hearts and minds to your Heavenly Father! God is waiting to meet you now!

NOVEMBER 29TH RUNNING FROM THE HEART

I will praise you, Lord my God, with all my heart; I will glorify your name forever. (Psalm 86:12 NIV)

Are you a runner of habit? Let's see if any of the following applies to you! 1. You run at the same time every day. 2. You wear the same or equivalent brand of socks, shoes, or clothing. 3. You cannot run unless you have music. 4. You always want to run the same route. 5. You cannot run unless you do the same pre-warm up routine. Okay, so maybe some or none of the above applies to you, but it is easy to see how running becomes automatic!

Do you know what else can become habitual? Worship! Sometimes our praise, reverence, and adorations for our King can become run of the mill, routine, and repetitious. It's time that we do more than numbly repeat what we read on a screen but worship our Creator from within, deep within our hearts that are bursting over with love and exaltation! Exalt God with all of your heart! Let your songs and words of praise explode from your mouth as though your very lungs would burst if God's praise stayed cooped up inside!

NOVEMBER 30ᵀᴴ SPICING UP YOUR RUN

Love the LORD your God with all your heart and with all your soul and with all your strength. (Deuteronomy 6:5 NIV)

Has running lost its sparkle? Perhaps you find yourself as bored as a gourd with running are robotically "running through" the motions! Is it time to mix things up? Let's get this workout party started with something new; such as running somewhere new, changing your running time frame, or listening to upbeat and encouraging music! Maybe it's time to find a friend to run alongside or train in a running group! Better yet, sign up for a race! Attack your staleness with something bold and new, like your first race!

Just like sprucing up your run, is it time to make some bold moves in your faith? Do not let luminous joy for serving God grow dim! Venture out and do something new and daring! Like walking up to a total stranger and sharing the gospel in the supermarket! Yes, give it a try! Go on that mission trip! Lead a small group! It can be amazing what God is waiting to do through you when you step out in faith. Step up and step out!

DECEMBER 1ˢᵀ RUNNING WITH HOLIDAY FEVER

For the grace of God has appeared that offers salvation to all people. It teaches us to say "No" to ungodliness and worldly passions, and to live self-controlled, upright and godly lives in this present age, (Titus 2:11-12 NIV)

Hello sugar cookie! Oh how I've missed you! One cookie, two cookies, three cookies, four cookies down the ol' hatch! How do you stay focused on your running and faithful to a heart healthy diet when your sweet tooth is surrounded by, not only your friends and family, but tempting pies, mouth watering cakes, sugary drinks, and chocolate treats that call your name! What can be your secret holiday tool? Self control!

Self restraint is not only important for holiday training and waist lines but for our everyday lives! Hold true and fast to the person God has created you to be! Stay focused on God's Word and how He has commanded us to live! This means saying yes to the life that was redeemed by the blood of Christ and no to the wants, wishes, and wanes of the world! It's not always easy but you have help! Call on God!

DECEMBER 2ND A RUNNING STANDSTILL

"I am the gate; whoever enters through me will be saved. They will come in and go out, and find pasture." (John 10:9 NIV)

What's holding you back? What is hindering your decision to start running? What obstacle is stopping you from jumping off the blocks and running that race? Maybe you are sold out for running but still on the fence about Jesus.

Perhaps you have been parked in a pew at church your whole life or have heard about God since you were a small child. However, you have never made that life changing decision to become a believer. But today is your day!

Today, just like any other day, you can become a child of God and have the promise of everlasting life. Today is your day to accept Jesus as your Lord and Savior. To trust, love, and obey God wholeheartedly and passionately. So if you still have one foot on one side of the fence and other dangling in the ways of the world, it's time to jump off the fence and into a new life that is only found in Christ!

DECEMBER 3RD POSTPONED

God is not unjust; he will not forget your work and the love you have shown him as you have helped his people and continue to help them. (Hebrews 6:10 NIV)

Feel like just skipping your run today and saving your workout for another date? You are not alone in wanting to just postpone! It can be quite easy to delay running when you are already dog-tired from the day alone! That being said, just as quickly as it is to toss aside your running plans and sit down and grab a snack, it is as easy to "overlook" and skip your calling to serve.

We often push off our responsibilities to help in our church or in the community to another day. But Christ has called you! Today! God has chosen you for a special purpose and plan! You are important to God's kingdom work and He needs the skills and talents He has placed uniquely inside of you! So don't delay and sign up today! You never know how much you will be blessed until you get moving!

DECEMBER 4TH THE MORE YOU RUN WITH JESUS

Jesus replied, "Anyone who loves me will obey my teaching. My Father will love them, and we will come to them and make our home with them." (John 14:23 NIV)

The more we run with Jesus, the more we learn to rely on Him. The more we run with Jesus daily the more we experience His goodness, mercy, and faithfulness. The more we run side by side with Jesus the more we learn to trust Him. As we learn to trust Jesus the more we lean on Him for strength. To run with Jesus is to realize the abundance of His faithfulness. We discover God's love, which is so deep, ever abundant, and continually overflowing. His mercy is everlasting.

In the weakness of our steps we realize our dependence on God's strength. We cannot run without Him. We need Jesus, He is our everything. To know our Messiah is to love Him. To seek our Savior is to find Him. The more we love Jesus the more we want to run right beside Him! Run today in the shadow of Christ's mercy!

DECEMBER 5ᵀᴴ TRUST THE TRAINING PLAN

"For I know the plans I have for you," declares the LORD, "plans to prosper you and not to harm you, plans to give you hope and a future." (Jeremiah 29:11 NIV)

The big day has finally arrived! Your faithful training has paid off. You nervously and very excitedly toe the starting line. As you wait, your mind starts to wander. Will you really be able to finish? That's a whole lot of miles. Maybe you didn't train long enough or vigorously enough! What if you do not make that time you have dreamed about? Worse yet, what if you cannot even finish?

In life, our mind often floods with worry. God has a plan for you in your life! A plan you can trust. So even when life gets rocky, you can have confidence! Confidence in The One who not only loves you but who also created you! We might not always be able to understand the plan but we can always trust God. We can rest assuredly in God's love. So even when you cannot see through the light at the end of the tunnel, remember that the God of the universe not only sees all but knows all!

DECEMBER 6ᵀᴴ RUNNING WITH HIGH EXPECTATIONS

"But seek first his kingdom and his righteousness, and all these things will be given to you as well." (Matthew 6:33 NIV)

Runners dream big! That's what we do! However, we at times can run with highly unrealistic expectations. Most runners already have a go getter type personality. So when we strive to reach a goal by the skin of our teeth, but end up falling fall short, that failure can be heart breaking. We begin to interrogate ourselves. "Why was I not fast enough?" "Why didn't I work harder"? The questions and the guilt can overwhelm us.

In our Christian walk we can do the same thing. We place these gigantic expectations on our shoulders and then feel utterly defeated when we fall short. But who told you that you had to be the best and achieve at everything? No one did! And our great God did not either. God loves you just as you are, for who you are.

As a child of God we have the freedom to live free. Free of unrealistic, burdensome expectations that we and others place upon our shoulders. We are to seek only one thing and one thing only. God! To live for God and glorify Him using the skills and abilities God has blessed us with. You are talented! Believe it.

DECEMBER 7ᵀᴴ RUNNING FROM WITHIN

There is one body and one Spirit, just as you were called to one hope when you were called; one Lord, one faith, one baptism; one God and Father of all, who is over all and through all and in all. (Ephesians 4:4-6 NIV)

You've got it. Yes you! You have what it takes to be a runner. A great one at that! You own the drive and the power! So run like you know it! Run knowing that you can do it! That you are tough enough! That nothing and no one can hold you back from running your dream. Guess what else you can do? Live!

Live life knowing that no matter who you are or what you have done, you have a Father in heaven who loves you. Who has forgiven you because of what His perfect Son did on the cross. Now God is living in you! Yes you right now! You have the power of the Holy Spirit dwelling in you as soon as you accept Jesus as your Lord and Savior. So live like it! Live knowing that The One who is over all and through all is living inside you! You can live triumphantly! Freely! Joyously!

DECEMBER 8ᵀᴴ INFLUENTIAL RUNNERS

Follow God's example, therefore, as dearly loved children and walk in the way of love, just as Christ loved us and gave himself up for us as a fragrant offering and sacrifice to God. (Ephesians 5:1-2 NIV)

You have been given an amazing opportunity! The unique opportunity all runners are given: to share Jesus with those who run beside you. Yep, this is your chance! Do not pass it up! As a runner you are blessed with the possibly of reaching others because of your running platform. As runners, we can pause and share the love of Jesus with everyone from those you "run into" in your local shoe shop, gym, sidewalks, trails, and parks.

As well as sharing the hope to which you run, to anyone who asks! We all have circles of influence, don't we? Probably in even more areas than we think! Let's just start to brainstorm all the places where God can use us to spread His love today; like your job, your home, your friends, your hobbies, your neighbors, within your favorite stores and restaurants, clubs or organizations you attend, sporting events, and your extended family. Whew! That's a whole lot of places and that's just naming a few! It's time to run and get busy spreading the love of Jesus today!

DECEMBER 9ᵀᴴ LIPS ON THE RUN

The LORD detests lying lips, but he delights in people who are trustworthy. (Proverbs 12:22 NIV)

Imagine you are sitting around lunch with your fellow co-workers. You are all contently munching on delicious sandwiches when the conversation turns to running. A couple long time runners begin to chime in with their staggering miles this week. Curious about yours, they begin to prod you. In response, you respond with a number that was actually double your actual amount. But this week you had actually been super busy and you barely ran at all, but they don't know that. Plus if it would have been a normal week, you would have easily ran that much. It can be easy to stretch the truth can't it? Especially when we try to be the big dog on top!

However, how often after we have covered up the truth, for whatever reason, do we start to feel uneasy, panged by our exaggerations! We are called to use our words in ways that are truthful, loving, and to build each other up in Christ! Our words are an extension of our hearts, so let them overflow with the love we have for God and for others!

DECEMBER 10ᵀᴴ SETTING RUN-ABLE GOALS

The plans of the diligent lead to profit as surely as haste leads to poverty. (Proverbs 21:5 NIV)

Setting goals is important! Aspirations keep runners focused, motivated, and hungry to achieve your goal! What are your running ambitions? Do you envision yourself completing your first marathon? Maybe your goals are not on a race but a number on the scale, a pant size, or a clean bill of health. So you have set running goals but what are your dreams for your life?

There are so many things we can do as members of the body of Christ! The sky is the limit and the people around you a sea of opportunities! So set some hopeful dreams for you in your life! Maybe God is calling you to invite a new person to church every Sunday, reach at least one soul with the gospel monthly, or go on that mission trip you have been dreaming about! Whatever you do, do it to glorify your Father in heaven! Happy goal setting!

DECEMBER 11ᵀᴴ YOU ARE AN OVERCOMER!

For everyone born of God overcomes the world. This is the victory that has overcome the world, even our faith. Who is it that overcomes the world? Only the one who believes that Jesus is the Son of God. (1 John 5:4-5 NIV)

You are an over comer! Yes you! Runners must overcome any number of hurdles that block their destination. Road blocks can be just about anything; from a scary medical diagnosis to someone telling you that you will never be able to run again.

Every day we face challenges that we choose to run and conquer or sit down in defeat. These deterrents can be both physical (finances or layoffs at work) to mental (worry or loneliness). However, as Christians we know we are assured of one thing! We do not have to go over these hurdles alone. God is with us, through Him we can win! We are over comers through Christ who saved us! So be strong and take courage! You do not have to run this race solo! Give your obstacle to God right now and run confidently beside Him!

DECEMBER 12ᵀᴴ LOVE RUNNING?

You, God, are my God, earnestly I seek you; I thirst for you, my whole being longs for you, in a dry and parched land where there is not water. (Psalm 63:1 NIV)

Moment of truth: do you actually love running or do you just run to reap its great benefits like losing those pesky holiday pounds? You are a runner no matter if you find running exhilarating or excruciating. But here's an even more serious moment of truth: are you living your life without truly loving God?

When you take a true look into your heart can you authentically say that it is full of adoration and passion for God and serving Him? God wants us to seek a relationship out of joy and love, not out of forced, unreal submission. God's love is so wide and so deep it is more than our human minds can ever fathom. God loves you just as you are. No matter where you are or what you have done. So live in a way that seeks God with all your heart, soul, and mind. May there be so much love in your heart for God, that you are an overflowing fountain of love. Bubbling compassion and charity for everyone to see!

DECEMBER 13ᵀᴴ IF YOU RUN HERE, I WILL RUN THERE

For the LORD your God is God of gods and LORD of lords, the great God, mighty and awesome, who shows no partiality and accepts no bribes. (Deuteronomy 10:17 NIV)

"God, if you will do this… I will do that…" Have you ever said this to God?

Perhaps it went something like this… "God if you help me finish this race, I will give to that charity." Or "God if you would just heal this injury I will be completely devoted to You."

Whatever that conversation might have sounded like, many of us can admit we have tried to manipulate God with either our words or our actions.

But aren't we forgetting God owns everything? God has created everything and everything is under His control. We have nothing that we could give God that He does not already have. What He is interested in is your heart! So give God your whole heart today and desire to do the will of Him who created you, no if, ands, or buts about it!

DECEMBER 14TH LITTLE FEET

Jesus said, "Let the little children come to me, and do not hinder them, for the kingdom of heaven belongs to such as these." (Matthew 19:14 NIV)

Run run run run…Run run run run…Run run run run. Who's this nonstop form of constant energy? Kids! Is today the day you take time to run with the child God has lovingly placed in your life? Together you can run around the play ground, circles around the backyard, or on a soccer field with a kickball. Playing with your daughter, son, niece, nephew, or grandchild is a perfect way to get your running workout in!

Making a positive impact in a young boy or girl's life is so important. The most important thing you can do for any child is to share the good news of God's love. Share with them how much God loves them and how important they are to God. Live your life in a way that points every precious soul to Jesus!

DECEMBER 15TH SHORT CUT

"Keep this Book of the Law always on your lips; meditate on it day and night, so that you may be careful to do everything written in it. Then you will be prosperous and successful." (Joshua 1:8 NIV)

You apprehensively glance at your wristwatch. You still have two and half miles to go. You anxiously wipe your brow. You could easily turn around and head home now and finish your favorite television show or you could faithfully finish your run. You hit the pause button on your watch and restlessly run in place.

What do you do?

This example might seem silly but how often do you cut short your time with God because of something as trivial as an evening TV program? Cutting it short has two major pitfalls, first we do not get the full time with God and second it can produce a pattern of spending less and less time reading God's Word and in prayer. It can be difficult to faithfully spend time with your Heavenly Father, especially when life gets hectic. However, it's time to stop taking short cuts and instead make time to be in His loving presence today.

DECEMBER 16TH RUNNING IN FEAR

There is no fear in love. But perfect love drives out fear, because fear has to do with punishment. The one who fears is not made perfect in love. (1 John 4:18 NIV)

Are you running in fear? Fear of gaining weight, fear of becoming injured, fear of an "imperfect" body image, or fear of failure?

We all have fears, but are you letting your fears get in the way of living? Are you letting your fears control your life? We sometimes even let fear stop us from serving God. We fear the opinions of others. We fear what they might say if we share our faith. We fear going on a mission trip. We fear teaching a Bible study. We fear stepping out in our faith. But there is no fear in love! God didn't make us to fear but to trust! Yes, that's easier said than done! However, just like running, we can begin to trust God one step at a time. So take that first step. God who is faithful and truly proves His trustworthiness again and again! If you trust Jesus with your salvation and eternal life, what fear is more important than that?

DECEMBER 17TH RUNNING WITH A HUMBLE HEART

Do nothing out of selfish ambition or vain conceit. Rather, in humility value others above yourselves, (Philippians 2:3 NIV)

Scoping out your competition? Without even knowing it, we all probably do the exact same thing, size up our competition! We all do!

In life, it can be hard not to compare ourselves to others. We judge others based on what they wear, how they speak, and where they live. How often we skip right over their hearts and cast our judgment on them, but God doesn't. God cares a lot about what's in our hearts. God desires for us to live in a way that places others over ourselves. God commands us to treat everyone around us with love and respect, just like we would want to be treated! So regard others with the love you wish to be shown! Run as servants of The One True God, overflowing with the love and joy of His love.

"Be completely humble and gentle; be patient, bearing with one another in love." (Ephesians 4:2 NIV)

DECEMBER 18ᵀᴴ THE PERSISTENT RUNNER

Then Jesus told his disciples a parable to show them that they should always pray and not give up. (Luke 18:1 NIV)

You spot it in the distance. The eagerly sought after and highly celebrated finish line. You can almost taste its nearness. You relentlessly dig in and quicken your pace to the melodies of encouragement and cheers from the lips and smiles of well-wishers flooded around the runner's path. Mouth dry and hands shaking you press into your run. A mixture of doubt and confidence welling inside your chest as you inhale a refreshing breath and focus on the goal ahead. In Luke 18, Jesus told a parable of a very persistent widow to teach us how to pray.

Does your persistence in running crossover to your prayer life? Do you relentlessly and unceasingly bring your prayers before your Heavenly Father? Bring your worries, your thoughts, and your praises to the King of kings. Keep praying!

DECEMBER 19ᵀᴴ I'M IN TRAINING

Have nothing to do with godless myths and old wives' tales; rather, train yourself to be godly. For physical training is of some value, but godliness has value for all things, holding promise for both the present life and the life to come. (1 Timothy 4:7-8 NIV)

If you are currently in training for an upcoming race or have completed one in the past, you understand how consuming training can be. It takes massive dedication, wholehearted passion, and a heavy commitment. Runners in training stick to a strict schedule, do their best to eat healthy (hello fruits and veggies), and of course running! A whole lot!

As a Christian we are also in training. We are in training, as followers of Jesus, to become more like Him. This conditioning is not for the faint of heart and also requires total dedication. As a follower of Christ, we must learn to say no to the things and to the desires that compete with our time and energy. Focus on the task at hand, living a life devoted to Christ! So stay focused, train diligently, and stay sharp because great is your reward in heaven!

DECEMBER 20TH RUN FOR HIM

If anyone speaks, they should do so as one who speaks the very words of God.
If anyone serves, they should do so with the strength God provides, so that in all
things God may be praised through Jesus Christ. To him be the glory and the power for ever and ever. Amen." (1 Peter 4:11a NIV)

If we are honest we can admit that as runners, running can be a bit of a selfish
sport. But the great news is it doesn't have to be that way! Anything can be turned
from a personal pursuit to a God honoring offering. When we take whatever our
hands and feet find to do and we do that thing to glorify God, we worship and
honor His name!

If you run, run for the Lord. Give that time, give that effort, and give thanks
for your ability to God. When others ask why you run, give that glory to your Maker. God put that fire, desire, and ability in you and only He fully deserves all credit.
If you cook, cook in a way that honors God. If you clean, praise God. If you clock
in at a job, work in a way that brings glory to your Father in heaven. Remember,
everything you do, do it for your Savior who saved you!

DECEMBER 21ST BRAVE FEET

Be strong and take heart, all you who hope in the LORD. (Psalm 31:24 NIV)

You can do this! You can do whatever you put your brave feet to do! You can
run that race. You can train for that goal. You can ultimately do anything you put
your heart to!

God has given you a great life. No matter what your circumstances or what
your past might look like, you are blessed! God loves you so much more than you
could ever hope or imagine and He wants all of you! God desires you to give Him
your everything, your all.

You have bold feet! You can do whatever God has placed in your heart to
do. No matter what others say or regardless of what you tell yourself. You are so
much more to God! You are a truly special treasure! Be courageous and bold! Your
strength is not in yourself but in your Creator who gives you strength! Run tall.
Be strong and believe! Believe in The One who paid it all so that you may have
life in Him!

DECEMBER 22ᴺᴰ RUNNING UP IN LIGHTS

"You are the light of the world. A town built on a hill cannot be hidden. Neither do people light a lamp and put it under a bowl. Instead they put it on its stand, and it gives light to everyone in the house." (Matthew 5:14-15 NIV)

Blueberry blues, sunshine yellows, poinsettia reds, olive greens, and plum purples brightly glimmer against the starry night. You reminiscently run along the street decked out in your finest cold weather gear. The snowflakes drop tranquilly on your rosy cheeks, pink nose, and snow kissed eyelashes. The street remains peaceful and calm revealing the grandeur of Christmas lights sweetly lightening your way up and down the streets. Running during the Christmas season creates some of the most memorable and enjoyable runs of the year.

Like the rainbow of colors that illuminate a holiday night, is a Christian who is the gleaming light of Christ within the world! We are to live as luminous lights pointing to Christ for any and all to see. We are to live as shining examples eagerly directing everyone to the Light of the world. Shine on! Write Christ's name in lights on our hearts and lives!

DECEMBER 23ᴿᴰ RUNNING IN HOPE

"She will give birth to a son, and you are to give him the name Jesus, because he will save his people from their sins." (Matthew 1:21 NIV)

Is Jesus the reason you run? Do you run with the hope you have in Christ? Jesus is the reason we can run as a courageous and unashamed runner! Is Jesus the reason you wake up in the morning with joy?

Jesus is the reason we have hope. Jesus is the reason we have peace. Jesus is the reason you have life even after you die. In a second, everything can change. It just takes one phone call, one life changing piece of news. One moment that can change your whole world, but when your hope is rooted firmly in Jesus, you can have peace! You can have peace knowing that no matter what happens you are a forgiven and saved child of God. So who is Jesus to you? Is Jesus your everything?

DECEMBER 24ᵀᴴ THE GIFT OF RUNNING

For the wages of sin is death, but the gift of God is eternal life in Christ Jesus our Lord. (Romans 6:23 NIV)

Open your present! That's right, peel back the elegantly wrapped silver bag and pull aside the glittery tissue paper. What is inside? Running! Running is a generous gift from God! You get to run because God blesses you with the gift of

running. God put the breath iny our lungs, the feet to take you, and the determination and desire to carry you through. Every precious step you take on your run is
a gift from your Father above.

In the same way, as a believer in Jesus Christ you have received the most important gift of all…eternal life! That's right, when you accept Jesus as your Lord
and Savior; you received the free gift of salvation. This beautiful gift of life is only
given through faith in Jesus and through Him alone!

DECEMBER 25ᵀᴴ RUNNING WITH GOOD NEWS OF GREAT JOY

The shepherds returned, glorifying and praising God for all the things they had
heard and seen, which were just as they had been told. (Luke 2:20 NIV)

Your breath heavily hangs in the clear air as you run outside, crisply romping
through the picturesque snow. It's a beautiful night and the stars are shining brightly through the cloudless night.

Hmm…reminds us of that field where some unsuspecting shepherds were
watching their flocks that night, when an angel of the Lord appeared to them,
announcing the glorious birth of our Savior. We all know and love the cherished
story of the birth of our Messiah but what will you do with the good news of great
joy? So who can you "go and tell?"

"When they had seen him, they spread the word concerning what had been
told them about this child, and all who heard it were amazed at what the shepherds
said to them." (Luke 2:17-18 NIV)

DECEMBER 26ᵀᴴ RUNNING REMINDERS

For the word of God is alive and active. Sharper than any double-edged sword,
it penetrates even to dividing soul and spirit, joints and marrow; it judges the
thoughts and attitudes of the heart. (Hebrews 4:12 NIV)

Beep! Beep! Beep! Your alarm nosily breaks the silence. You yawn as you
clamor out of your warm sheets and step onto the floor. As you head for your coffee maker, you instantly spot your daily workout reminder, your running shoes!
That's right; your shoes are set in the perfect position, where they will be one of
the first things you see when you wake up. They sit there in wait, to usher you into
today's adventure!

Just as important as it is to set out your running shoes to ensure you run every
day, it is as vital for you to expertly place your Bible. Keep your Bible in a place
where you will be reminded daily not only to open its pages but have it within

arm's reach when you are in need of Him! Have God's Word ready and right where you can see it! Keep your sword drawn, ready, and prepared to fight!

DECEMBER 27TH IT'S OKAY TO ASK

The heart of the discerning acquires knowledge, for the ears of the wise seek it out. (Proverbs 18:15 NIV)

What is that? What is this? Feeling a little confused? You are not alone! Have you ever felt embarrassed to ask someone else a question because you feel like you should already know the answer? This happens all the time as a runner! Even though you might not be new to running, we tend to keep our burning questions to ourselves just because we don't want to look inexperienced!

Believers can feel much the same way. We can sometimes feel like we should know the answer to all the questions! But the real truth is that no one knows everything! Only God does! So it's okay to ask! That's what maturing in your faith is all about, discovering more and more about the awesome God we serve!

DECEMBER 28TH UNFORGIVING RUNNER

"Therefore, I tell you, her many sins have been forgiven- as her great love has shown. But whoever has been forgiven little loves little." (Luke 7:47 NIV)

Running can be unforgiving, painful, tiresome, and hard, on all its participants! Running expects runners to show up ready, prepared, and set to run! No excuses! Running is not an example of how we should act to those who have hurt us. But how often is it exactly how we act towards others!

We, who have been washed in the blood of Christ, sometimes refuse to let go of another neighbor's sin against us. When we act as an unyielding, immovable object, refusing to accept the grievances and faults done against us, we continue to suffer because we remain unforgiving. Is there someone in your life that you need to forgive today? Today is the day to forgive because through Christ, God forgave you! That pain you are feeling is too much to hold on to! Let go of your past hurts and pains! Forgive and boldly run on!

DECEMBER 29TH RUNNING IMPRESSIONS

"No one is like you, LORD; you are great, and your name is mighty in power." (Jeremiah 10:6 NIV)

Is your impression of running off track to how running truly is? Hmm… consider it for a second. Do you find yourself dreading your run but then once your workout is finished, you realize it wasn't that bad?

What about your perception of God? Could it be possible that your perception of God is different than how He actually is? Hmm, maybe you conceptualized God only as a condemning Father, someone who is looking to bring down the hammer the moment you mess up. Or perhaps you treat God in the totally opposite way and only view Him as someone who can bless you and treat you as you see fit. So maybe it's time we take a closer look at who God really is. Today is the day, to crack open God's Word and open its pages to discover who the Creator of the universe is and all He has done. It's time to take a closer look. God's Word sings of God's love, exudes forgiveness, overflows with grace, and shouts of God's power and greatness!

DECEMBER 30TH NEXT YEAR'S GAME PLAN

Commit to the LORD whatever you do, and he will establish your plans. (Proverbs 16:3 NIV)

Okay, its go time! We are just a day away from a new year and it's time to set our hopes and dreams for tomorrow. Every year offers new and exciting possibilities and opens opportunities to live for Christ! So what will your resolutions for a hopeful new year be? What kind of expectant wishes do you have excitedly planned? Take the time to write down goals for both running and most importantly for your Christian walk! Run your first five miles! Run your first marathon! Go on a mission trip! Start volunteering in your community! The skies are the limit and the earth is your starting place!

Dedicate this year to living and running for God with all your heart, soul, and mind! So what is it that God has laid on your heart to do within this brand new year? Pray that God gives you the boldness, the strength, and the courage to turn your plans for Him into a success! What will you do with the gift of a new year?

DECEMBER 31ST RUNNING RECAP!

"He guides me along the right paths for his name's sake." (Psalm 23:3b NIV)

Today is a day to celebrate and reflect on this beautiful year God has given you. There have been numerous changes both on the inside and on the outside. You have become a stronger, bolder runner! You are an inspiration to all! You have really come along and your confidence and courageousness exudes from you! Most importantly others can see Christ shining in and through you!

Look back and see all that God has been doing inside you to further His kingdom this past year! You are a unique and extraordinary special child of God and it is important to always remember that. God has an individual plan for you and you have a special mission to keep training for. So never give up, keep running on, and always remember that no matter what you are going through, God loves you! God is for you and He is always there to get you through! Run to glorify God!